COLLOQUIAL NEPALI

COLLOQUIAL NEPALI

G. G. ROGERS

GYAN

Published by

GYAN

Gyan Publishing House
5, Ansari Road
Daryaganj, New Delhi-110002
Phone: 011-47034999, 9811692060
E-mail: books@gyanbooks.com

Distribution Network
gyanbooks.com
India, USA, Canada, UK, Australia, France

ISBN : 978-81-212-4267-7 (PB)
First Published, Calcutta, 1950

2nd Impression 2020

Printed at: Gyan Press, Delhi.

PREFACE

THE sixty lessons contained in the following pages have been compiled from notes prepared by me when employed as Nepali Instructor with the Gurkha Brigade during the second World War. Many forms of the Nepali language exist in India and Nepal including firstly, a very cultured and pure form found in the central valley, sometimes termed the Court language, containing high-sounding phrases many of Sanskrit origin ; secondly, a form found in eastern and western Nepal and lastly, an extremely impure form of speech, being a regimental language containing at least 60% pure Hindustani words and construction, evolved for parade purposes. The form found in eastern Nepal slightly differs from, and is purer than, the western form.

My object in these pages is to put before the student a simple form of the language as spoken in eastern and western Nepal ; that is, a pure form of the language as used by the young soldier or recruit in any Gurkha regiment. It would obviously be futile, indeed impossible, to attempt to teach the mixed language known as " line bāt " referred to above. The young soldier does not know this form but gradually learns it on parade or at the orderly room but immediately reverts to his own speech when off parade. It varies considerably in different regiments and is certainly not standard. Regiments and individual Gurkhas domiciled in the Punjab, for instance, have included quite a number of Punjabi words and expressions in their speech. I am moreover convinced that it is highly desirable that officers should be able to speak a language which appeals to their men and which they really understand, and not merely a mixed language chiefly confined to the more senior Gurkha ranks, and even then only employed by them when speaking to non-Gurkhas in the fear that if they were to speak their own language they would not be understood. Where the eastern form is at variance with the western a note has been made to that effect.

As regards the general lay-out, the book consists of sixty lessons including certain lessons set aside for revision. Each lesson is designed to include sufficient work for one hour's study and at the end of a large number of lessons test sentences are given. The English sentences should be translated by the student without reference to the Nepali translation, in each case given after the English. The Nepali translations should then be used as a key by the student, enabling him to correct his own work. Many notes and explanations are included with these translations. Throughout the book, where alternative Nepali forms exist, they are shewn in brackets. In the vocabularies and sentences, in many cases, references are made to the lesson in which the particular phrase or word will be found explained. In the English-Nepali vocabulary the letter "v" indicates "verb". The letters "tr." and "intr." in brackets after a verb indicate "transitive" and "intransitive" and are only inserted when a doubt might arise. At the beginning of the majority of lessons a vocabulary is given of words to be used in the lesson or test sentences. If however a word or phrase is explained in a lesson it is not included in the vocabulary for that lesson and words once included in these vocabularies or explanations are not repeated at the beginning of subsequent lessons.

I cannot lay too much stress on the importance of really mastering the sounds explained in Lessons 2 and 3 before going on to other lessons. The learning of a language is the acquisition of the spoken utterance and unless a student can really acquire these sounds which may be quite strange to him he cannot hope to speak the language in an accent readily understandable by the young soldier. Indeed, his failure to imitate the exact sounds will always handicap him and will tend to prevent him from attaining any real fluency. I have found that in the teaching of foreign languages the importance of precise sound is sometimes not sufficiently stressed. The long *"ā"*, for instance, is often dismissed by the explanation that it represents the sound of the "a" in the English word "father". In point of fact it bears little resemblance to that sound. Its precise sound will be found explained in Lesson 2. Similarly the short *"a"* sound bears little resemblance to the "u" sound in the English word "but" and really has no corresponding English sound, though the "ir" sound in the English word "dirt" comes very close to it. There are of course many other sounds not included in Lessons 2 and 3, but as they approximate to similar English sounds they have not been mentioned. No attempt has been made to explain the difference between the sound of the hard *"d"*, *"r"*, and *"t"* and their soft counterparts as it is considered that this can only be acquired by practice after hearing the sounds actually uttered. The cardinal importance of making syllables end on vowel sounds, as fully explained in Lesson 2, should never be lost sight of. It is the key to acquiring the correct accent. Many students have told me that the realisation and practice of this important rule has helped them more than anything else to speak the language reasonably well.

In conclusion it must be explained that consequent on variations in the language the rendering of some Nepali words in the Roman script is more or less arbitrary. As an example, the Nepali word "*mān*"—"in" is pronounced "ma" in many parts of the country, and the word "*mānthi*"—"above", "on" is often rendered "*māthi*". By repeated checking of both manuscript and typescript every effort has been made to ensure that, as far as these pages are concerned, precisely the same rendering of the same word is always employed. If however any slight variance is found, as for instance, in the employment or otherwise of the nasal "*n*" in a certain word, I am confident that it will be realised that thousands of accents have had to be carefully checked and it is always possible that one or two may have been missed.

If this book helps to further understanding and sympathy for the Gurkha, both in the Army and in civil life, I shall be satisfied that my labours have not been in vain.

My thanks are due to Capt. J. Miller, late 2nd K. E. VII's O. Gurkhas for the help he gave me in tabulating the vocabularies, and to my wife for her invaluable help in typing the manuscript without which the production of the book would have been impossible.

G. G. Rogers,
Lieut.-Colonel,
late 1st K. G. V's O. Gurkha Rifles.

London, 1950.

CONTENTS

LESSON PAGE

LESSON 1

ON THE ART OF SPEAKING A FOREIGN LANGUAGE

1. To acquire a language is to learn the spoken utterance. The natural receptive medium is, therefore, the ear, not the eye. It is an art very much akin to music.

2. We therefore have to acquire pitch or tone, accent or correct pronunciation of sounds, and swing of natural beauty.

3. Certain difficulties exist which tend to prevent students from acquiring these things. These are:

(a) natural hesitation to speak in a tone or accent other than that of one's own language caused by

(i) a disinclination to act the part of someone else, partly caused by shyness, and

(ii) the fact that some people are unmusical and therefore find it difficult to imitate or mimic;

(b) a feeling that one's own accent is good enough and therefore why go to the trouble of imitating a foreign accent?

4. To speak a foreign language well, we must not entertain any of the above ideas. We must imitate and mimic the whole time. We must never imagine that our efforts will be laughed at. There are so many hundreds of dialects in India that speaking incorrectly does not sound so odd as it might in another country.

We must also fully understand that certain sounds exist in every language which do not exist in our own language. We must learn how to prdouce these sounds. Fortunately in *Nepali* the foreign sounds are very few, but we must learn them before attempting to speak. We must copy and imitate exact sounds made by the Gurkha. In order to do this we must *really* listen when a Gurkha is speaking. Some people are only half listening, i.e., they are not concentrated.

5. Lastly, we must never hesitate to talk, talk, talk on every possible occasion. The Gurkha will never laugh at our feeble attempts at the outset. On the contrary, he will be only too pleased to help us as much as possible. And while talking, we must act and mimic.

6. The chief reason for paying attention to phonetics is that if a student understands correct sounds he is not only more readily understood but he also learns much more quickly as he is hearing it the whole time.

LESSON 2

[This Lesson and the next one deal with ten sounds which are different to any English sounds and therefore must be mastered.]

I. Vowel Sounds

(a) *ā*: pronounced something like the American pronunciation of English *o*; example: a child's *doll* pronounced by Americans *dāll*. It is *not* the same sound as the *a* in *father*. To make the sound the extreme ends of the mouth have to be slightly drawn apart; special care is necessary to pronounce it long when it comes at the end of a word.

(b) *a* (without the long mark): This is the short *a*. It is pronounced like the *ir* in the English word *dirt*. A most important rule in regard to accent must be mentioned here, namely, that as the Nepali language is a phonetic language we must, whenever possible, break up words so that each syllable ends on a vowel sound. This is the reverse of English where, as far as possible, sounds or syllables are made to end on consonants. Take, for example, the place name, TRIPOLI. An Englishman pronounces this TRIP-OL-I, whereas a Frenchman would say TRI-PO-LI, which, in point of fact, is a far more logical pronunciation. This is also the Nepali pronunciation. *Pani* (ALSO) is pronounced *Pa-ni*, the short *a* in *pa* being pronounced like the *ir* in *dirt*. An Englishman not trained in these phonetics would naturally pronounce it *pan-i*, making the *pan* sound to rhyme with the English word *fun*. This is quite incorrect. Where we find two consonants together in the middle of a word it is obvious that we cannot normally make each sound end on a vowel. For instance, in *rāmro* (GOOD), the *m* becomes the final letter in the first syllable or sound, and the *r* the initial letter in the second sound. This rule does not refer to cases where *h* comes after a consonant, when it is pronounced with the consonant it follows, such as, *Gurkhāli*. First syllable is *Gur*, second syllable is *kha*, third syllable is *li*.

Practice: Long *ā—mā, tā, nā, bā, lā, dā*
ā-mā—MOTHER
lā-to—DUMB
ko-thā—A ROOM (Notice long *ā* here at end of word)

Short *a—ma, ta, na, ba, kă, la, da*
ban, bal, mal, man, das

Unless checked, a tendency here would be to pronounce *ban* like the English word *bun*. This is not correct. Pronounce short *a* like *ir* in *dirt*, thus *pa-ni*—as *pir-ni*.

(c) *e*: This sound is not very difficult provided that the student appreciates that it is an un-English sound. Pronounce it long and never like *ai* in the English *tail*.

Practice: *me, te, ne, be, ke, le, de*
mel, tel, met, Da-le (man's name)

(d) *i*: This sound is something like the cockney form of *he*, but a little longer. When coming at the end of a word or sound such as in *pāni* (WATER), there is a tremendous tendency to pronounce it like the final *y* in English, such as in the word *slowly*. This is quite incorrect.

Practice: *ti-mi*—YOU
pā-ni—WATER
et-ti—AS MANY AS THIS

A slightly shorter *i* sound also exists like the *i* in the English word *tin*.

Practice: *din, hin*

(e) *o*: This sound is very short, something like the French *o*. It must never be pronounced long like the sound in the English word *owe*.

Practice: *bo, to, ro, ko*
bol-nu, thu-lo, tol

(f) *u*: According to the present system of transliteration pronounced long like *oo* in English. It must never be pronounced short such as in the English *full*, and is, in fact, more like the *oo* sound in the English *fool*.

Practice: *mu, tu, nu, bu, ku*
bhuth—AN EVIL SPIRIT
dulnu—TO MOVE ABOUT, OT GO FOR A WALK

LESSON 3

2. Consonant Sounds

(a) *r*: This sound is very difficult for an English to pronounce, especially when it comes at the end of a syllable or word. It has to be definitely pronounced and very slightly rolled, being pronounced *ra* as in the first sound of *reliable.*

Example: *par-chha, dar* (FEAR), *chār* (FOUR), *tār* (A WIRE)
Ur-du (pronounced *oor-doo*), *bahādur, Lālbir*

Most English people fail to pronounce the final *r*; e.g., in the expression "stocks at *par*" the *r* of *par* is hardly pronounced; compare it with the English word *pa* (FATHER). In English very little *r* sound is made in words such as FAR, CAR, etc.

(b) *n* (nasal): written with a dot (*ṅ*), rather like a nasal grunt.

Example:	*māṅ*—IN, ON, AT, TO, etc.	*jāṅr*—RICE BEER
	maṅ—I	*hiṅrnu*—TO MOVE, WALK
	chiuṅro—CHIN	*kuṅrāghāt*—a place name
	duṅgā—BOAT	*sadhaiṅ*—ALWAYS
	(Note long *ā*)	*chāṅro*—QUICKLY

(c) *h*: When coming after a consonant it requires practice. If the *h* sound is ignored this invariably produces another word having another meaning.

Example:	*thio*—WAS	*dhungā*—A STONE
	tio—HE, SHE, IT	*duṅgā*—A BOAT
	dhān—RICE (growing)	*ghorā*—A HORSE
	dān—A GIFT	*gorā*—FAIR, WHITE

If difficulty is found, insert before the *h* whatever vowel comes after it. Thus, *ghorā* becomes *gohorā,* and in accordance with the method of splitting up sounds to make each end in a vowel as learnt in Lesson 2 we pronounce this *go-ho-rā,* making the *h* into an initial *h,* which is not difficult. We gradually learn with practice to shorten this to *ghorā.* It is purely a matter of practice.

3. The *ai* Sound

This sound is very common for strengthening or emphasising nouns, adjectives and verbs, and sometimes pronouns. Note carefully, it contains the short *a* sound and not the long *ā*. It is therefore pronounced *a-i* and not *ā-i*.

Example:	*rāmro*—GOOD	Strong form,	*rāmrai*
	thulo—BIG	,,	*thulai*
	timi—YOU	,,	*timinai*
	ghar—HOUSE	,,	*gharai*
	āunu parchha—HE MUST COME	,,	*āunai parchha*

In the spoken form of the language it is used very much.

NOTE: The *āi* sound is not common and is found in the past participles of verbs ending in *āunu*.

Example: *garāunu*—TO CAUSE TO DO
garāi, garāikana—HAVING CAUSED TO DO
āunu—TO COME
āi, āikana—HAVING COME

LESSON 4

VOCABULARY

forest—*ban*
to sit—*basnu*
at, on, in—*māṅ*
always—*sadhaiṅ*
to speak—*bolnu*
to say, tell—*bhannu*
work—*kām*
or—*ki*
meat—*māsu*
to move, shake (tr.)—*halāunu*
this—*yo*
that—*tio*
sunday—*āitwār*
house—*ghar*
room—*kothā*
to lie down—*sutnu*
day—*din*
every day—*dine piche*
own—*āphnu*
to move, shake (intr.)—*halinu*
evening—*beluki*
morning—*bihāno*
where?—*kahāṅ*
to where, whither?—*katā*
road—*bāto*
to walk, move—*hiṅrnu*
father—*bābu*
mother—*āmā*
to sleep—*nidhāunu*

The Conjugation of Verbs

NOTE I.—All verbs end in *nu*. Cut off the final *nu* and we have the stem or root to which terminations are added.

Exceptions:—Verbs ending in *inu* all of which are intransitive take back the *n* in the present habitual tense. Verbs ending in *āunu* or *ānu* do the same thing. The rule is, if a vowel comes before the *nu,* take back the *n* in the present habitual tense, e.g.,

ubhinu (intr.)—TO STAND	Present habitual root — *ubhin*
tarsinu (intr.)—TO FEAR	,, ,, ,, — *tarsin*
tarsāunu (tr.)—TO FRIGHTEN	,, ,, ,, — *tarsāun*
thuprinu (intr.)—TO BE COLLECTED	,, ,, ,, — *thuprin*
thuprāunu (tr.)—TO STACK, COLLECT	,, ,, ,, — *thuprāun*
garāunu (tr. caus.)—TO CAUSE TO DO	,, ,, ,, — *garāun*

All verbs ending in *inu* are intransitive.

Nearly all verbs ending in *āunu* are transitive.

NOTE 2.—Very few verbs have an ending in *ānu*, e.g.,

lānu—TO TAKE (WITH) *jānu*—TO GO

khānu—TO EAT *orhlānu*—TO DESCEND

But in "line bāt", that is, the form of speech employed by Gurkhas domiciled in India, we find a great tendency to make all verbs which should end in *āunu* end in *ānu* to bring the sounds into line with Urdu verbs, a great number of which end in *ānā* and none in *āunā* ; a large number of Nepali verbs do, however, end in *anu* (short *a*).

ACTIVE TRANSITIVE VERB: *garnu*—TO DO

PRESENT HABITUAL

I DO (not I AM DOING)

Maṅ gar-chhu—I DO
taṅ gar-chhas—THOU DOEST
u or *tio gar-chha*—HE, SHE, IT DOES

NOTE 1.—The second person singular always ends in *s* in the positive and negative except in the Aorist Tense.

NOTE 2.—The plural WE, YOU, THEY—*hami, timi,* and *uni* (THEY there), *ini* (THEY here) will not be given in any tense of the verb because in speech we use the terminations of the 3rd person singular in all persons of the plural. We may add the word *haru* to the pronoun in the plural and to any concrete noun in the plural, e.g.,

mānchhe haru—THE MEN

It is not usually added to abstract nouns, e.g.,
sāl—YEAR, also YEARS (not *sāl haru*)

NOTE 3.—The above tense cannot be used for the present non-habitual but can be used for the *near* future:

I WILL DO IT NOW—*maṅ āile garchhu*
HE WILL SIT HERE TO-MORROW—*u bholi yahāṅ baschha*

NEGATIVE OF PRESENT HABITUAL

maṅ gar-daina—I DO NOT DO
taṅ gar-dainas—THOU DOST NOT DO
u or *tio gar-daina*—HE DOES NOT DO

In the Present habitual with verbs having a vowel sound before the final *nu* take back the *n* of the *nu* to form the stem. In the negative the 'short' negative is employed, i.e., termination *na* in place of *daina* etc., e.g.,

u tarsin-na—HE DOES NOT FEAR
u ubhin-na—HE DOES NOT STAND
yahāṅ āun-na—HE DOES NOT COME HERE
u hun-na—HE IS NOT (habitual)

In **Eastern Nepali** there is a tendency to employ the long negative termination *daina* with these verbs.

In any question which cannot be answered by NO or YES, such as WHERE IS YOUR FATHER? We may add the sound *aṅ* to denote the question; The voice is slightly lowered when pronouncing it:

Timro bābu kahāṅ chha aṅ?

Sentences

ENGLISH

1. He lives in the forest.
2. We speak Gurkhāli.
3. They always do it.
4. Do you work?
5. They do not speak English.
6. He does not eat meat.
7. He does not stack (collect) the boots in this room.
8. He comes to Dehra Dun on Sundays.
9. He does not sleep in the house.
10. I do *not* go to my home every day.
11. Where do you go in the evening?
12. He walks along the road.
13. He speaks Gurkhāli.
14. He moves (habitually).

1. U ban māṅ baschha.
2. Hami Gurkhāli bolchha.
3. Uni (haru) sadhaiṅ garchha.
4. Taṅ kām garchhas ki?

   (NOTE: *ki* at the end of a sentence is short for *ki gardainas*, i.e., DO YOU WORK, OR DO YOU NOT WORK?)

5. Ini haru Angrezi boldaina.

SHORT NEGATIVE

6. U māsu khān-na.
7. Yo kothā māṅ boot haru thuprāun-na.

   (NOTE the tendency to leave out the pronoun in this language.)

8. Āitwār āitwār Dehra Dun māṅ āun-chha.
9. Ghar māṅ sutdaina (lit. DOES NOT LIE DOWN).
10. Maṅ dine piche (āphnu) ghar māṅ jān-na.
11. Timi beluki katā jān-chha?

    (NOTE: No *māṅ* after *beluki*. Note the use of *katā* with verbs of movement only, but *kahāṅ* may be used here and must be used with those verbs not indicating movement.)

12. U bāto bātai hiṅrchha.
13. U Gurkhāli bolchha.
14. U halinchha.

LESSON 5

VOCABULARY

to hear, listen—*sunnu*
bed—*khāt*
son—*choro*
daughter—*chori*
boy, young man—*tithā*, (E) *ketā*
children—*ketā keti*
small—*sāno*, *siāno*
field—*bāri*
dog—*kukur*
to hit—*hānnu*
cat—*birālu*
man, person—*mānchhe*
to eat—*khānu*
valley—*kholsā*
to descend—*jharnu*
to ascend, climb—*charhnu*
to run—*dugurnu*
up, upwards—*umbho*
down, downwards—*undho*
ground—*bhuin*

IMPERFECT INDICATIVE

I WAS DOING

Maiṅ le gariāko thieṅ—I WAS DOING
taiṅ le gariāko this—THOU WAST DOING
u or *ti le gariāko thio*—HE WAS DOING

(Pronoun in Agent Case—BY ME, BY THEE, BY HIM.)

RULE—*Transitive Verbs*: The pronoun must be in the Agent Case in past tenses or when past participle is used. It may be in the Agent Case in other tenses if it is desired to emphasise the pronoun.

Intransitive Verbs: The pronoun is never in the Agent Case. *Gariāko* is really a form of the past participle. In the Western form we leave out the *ko* when speaking only, but not in writing. In writing we usually find *garieko* and not *gariāko*; but always use *gariāko* when speaking.

Eastern Nepali has a form of this tense:
maṅ garde thieṅ, taṅ garde this, u garde thio

This form is also used in Western Nepal but means here HE WAS IN THE ACT OF DOING and has not therefore the normal Imperfect Tense meaning WAS DOING. Note also the strong form of this tense; *maṅ gardā thieṅ.*

NEGATIVE

I WAS NOT DOING, ETC.

maiṅ le gariāko thina
taiṅ le gariāko thinas
u le gariāko thina

Note the *s* at the end of the negative second person.

Eastern Nepali: *maṅ garde thina*
taṅ garde thinas
u garde thina

Sentences

ENGLISH

1. They were listening to me.
2. They were sitting on the bed.
3. The daughter of the mother was eating.
4. The boy was not walking on the road.
5. He was sleeping on the bed.

6. You were speaking.
7. He was standing in the field.
8. He was hitting the dog.
9. Where (whither) was he running?
10. The cat was not sitting on the bed.
11. The men were going down into the valley.

Nepali

1. Uni haru maṅ lāi suniā(ko) thio. (*Eastern*: sunde thio).
2. Uni haru khāt māṅ basiā ko thio.

   (Note: *Māṅ*—IN, INSIDE, ON, AT, TO (in regard to locality), *Dehra Dun māṅ*—TO DEHRA DUN, *Lāi*—TO, *le*—BY, *ko*—OF.)

3. Āmā ko chori khā (ko) thio.
4. Tithā bāto māṅ hiṅriā (ko) thina. (*Eastern*: Ketā—Eastern word for BOY—bāto māṅ hiṅrde thina.)
5. U khāt māṅ nidhāko thio. (*Eastern*: nidhāunde thio.)

   (Note that the Past Participles of verbs ending in *āunu* take the long *ā* only, *not iā*; i.e., cut off the *u* as well as the *nu*; e.g.,

āyāko (*āko*)	Past Participle	of	*āunu*—TO COME
garāko	,, ,,	of	*garāunu*—TO CAUSE TO DO
thuprāko	,, ,,	of	*thuprāunu*—TO STACK OR COLLECT)

6. Timi boliā(ko) thio. (*Eastern*: Timi bolde thio.)
7. U bāri māṅ ubhiā(ko) thio.
8. U le kukur hāniā(ko) thio.
9. U katā (kahāṅ) duguriāko thio? (*Eastern*: U katā dugurde thio?)
10. Birālu khāt māṅ basiā(ko) thina.
11. Mānchhe haru kholsā māṅ jhariā(ko) thio. (undho gā(ko) thio).

    (Note: *Umbho*—UPWARDS *Undho*—DOWNWARDS)

LESSON 6

VOCABULARY

to-day—*āju*
yesterday—*hijo*
nowadays—*hijo āju*
the day after to-morrow—*parsi*
shortly, in a few days' time—*bholi parsi*
to-morrow—*bholi*
the day before yesterday, the other day—*asti*
some time ago—*hijo asti*
to reach, suffice—*pugnu*
to arrive—*āipugnu*
how? in what manner?—*kasori?*
in that manner—*tesori*
to fall (*from a height*)—*khasnu*
to overbalance (intr.)—*paltinu*
to cause to overbalance (tr.)—*paltāunu*
soldier—*sipāhi*
hill—*dāṅrā*
on, above—*māṅthi*
river—*kholā*
to play—*khelnu*
why?—*kina, kelāi*
night—*rāt*
at night—*rāti*
leave—*bidā*
speech, talk, language, thing—*kurā*
bag, sack—*borā, bori*
to take up, hold—*linu*
towards—*tira*
to retire—*hatnu*
tree—*rukh*
branch—*hāṅgā*
to bring—*liāunu, liera āunu*
to advance, increase (intr.)—*barhnu*
to increase (tr.)—*barhāunu*
flour—*pitho*
parade—*kawāz*
hand, arm—*hāth*
bird—*charā*

PAST INDICATIVE

I DID

As this is a past tense of a transitive verb the pronoun *must* be in the Agent Case.

Maiṅ le garieṅ—I DID
taiṅ le garis—THOU DIDST
u le gario—HE DID

It should be noted here that although this tense grammatically means I DID, it is often used to mean I HAVE DONE provided the DOING is completed, e.g., *āyo Gurkhāli*—THE GURKHAS HAVE COME

NEGATIVE

maiṅ le garina
taiṅ le garinas
u le garina

THE PERFECT TENSE

I HAVE DONE
(=I AM DOING in English)

This is the tense we use for the Present Non-Habitual. Provided an action has commenced, even if it is not completed, this tense may be used. The sentence THE MEN ARE SITTING OUTSIDE THE ROOM is considered to be in the past tense because the action of sitting is complete, i.e., although in English we say ARE SITTING, in Nepali they say HAVE SAT because the action has already commenced, indeed in this case is complete. As the tense is actually a past tense the pronoun must be in the Agent Case.

maiṅ le gariā(ko) chhu—I HAVE DONE
taiṅ le gariā(ko) chhas—THOU HAST DONE
u le gariā(ko) chha—HE HAS DONE

The colloquial form of the 3rd person is *gari chha* which may be used in speech with all verbs having a stem ending in a consonant.

NEGATIVE

maiṅ le gariāko chhaina
taiṅ le gariāko chhainas
u le gariāko chhaina

Eastern Nepali of this Present Non-Habitual is:

maiṅ gardai chhu
taiṅ gardai chhas
u gardai chha

and so on.

Westerners also employ this form but only in the sense of IN THE ACT OF, IN PROCESS OF.

Sentences

ENGLISH

1. He reached Saharanpur yesterday.
2. How did you overbalance?
3. The Gurkhas arrived the other day.
4. The soldiers climbed the hill.
5. The bird fell to the ground.
6. The company of Japs went down to the river.
7. The children played football this morning.

8. He did the work yesterday.
9. Why did that Gurkha go to-day?
10. Where did you go last night?
11. He has gone on leave to Nepal.
12. He spoke to the recruits.
13. The sahabs are sitting in the Mess.
14. The company of enemy is retiring.
15. The birds are sitting in the branches of the trees.
16. No. 7 Platoon is advancing.
17. He is bringing the bag of flour to my house.
18. The men are going on parade.
19. He is holding his rifle in his hand.

NEPALI

1. U hijo Sahāranpur māṅ pugio.
2. Taṅ kasori paltis?
3. Gurkhāli haru asti āipugio.
4. Sipāhi haru dāṅrā māṅthi charhio.

(NOTE: *dāṅrā māṅthi*—TOP OF THE HILL;
dāṅrā māṅ—ON THE HILL.)

5. Charā bhuiṅ māṅ khasio.
6. Jāpan ko kampani kholā māṅ jhario.

(NOTE: *kholā tira jhario*—IN THE DIRECTION OF THE RIVER is very common and good Nepali.)

7. Ketā keti haru le āju bihāno football khelio.
8. U le hijo kām gario.
9. Tio Gurkhāli āju kina gayo (go) aṅ?
10. Āju rāti katā gais aṅ?
11. U bidā māṅ Gurkhā māṅ go (gayo)
12. U rakrut haru sita kurā gario.
13. Sāhab haru mess kot māṅ basiā(ko) chha.
14. Jāpan ko kampani hatiā(ko) chha.
15. Charā haru rukh ko hāṅgā māṅ basiā(ko) chha.
16. Sāt platoon 'advance' gariā(ko) chha [(ko) "barhiā(ko)" chha]
17. U pitho ko borā mero ghar māṅ haru achha. (ako chha)
18. Mānchhe haru kawāz māṅ gā(ko) chha.
19. Rifle hāth māṅ liā(ko) chha.

LESSON 7

VOCABULARY

pit—*khālto*
to dig—*khannu*
once, twice, etc.—
ek pāli, dui pāli, etc.
shop, bazar—*pasal*
shop-keeper—*pasale*
to cross (intr.)—*tarnu*
to take across (tr.)—*tārnu*
to jump over, cross—*nāngnu*
bone—*hār*
wall—*bhittā*
office—*daftar*

PAST PERFECT

I HAD DONE

maiṅ le gariā(ko) thieṅ—I HAD DONE
taiṅ le gariā(ko) this—THOU HADST DONE
u le gariā(ko) thio—HE HAD DONE

NEGATIVE

maiṅ le gariā(ko) thina—I HAD NOT DONE
taiṅ le gariā(ko) thinas—THOU HADST NOT DONE
u le gariā(ko) thina—HE HAD NOT DONE

The student will be surprised that precisely the same form is used here as in the Imperfect, I WAS DOING. The fact is that colloquially the same form is used meaning I WAS DOING and I HAD DONE ; in other words, the Past Tenses are interchangeable ; the Perfect, I HAVE DONE being reserved for the Non-Habitual Present.

Sentences

ENGLISH

1. He had dug a pit in the field.
2. The Subadar had told them three times.
3. The shop-keepers had come to the office.
4. He had crossed the river.
5. The men had jumped over the wall.
6. The dog had eaten the bone.

1. U bārī mān khālto khaniā ko thio.
2. Subadār Sāhab le uni haru lāi tin pāli bhaniā(ko) thio.
3. Pasale haru daftar mān ā(ko) thio.
4. Kholā tariā(ko) thio.
5. Mānchhe haru le bhittā nāngiā(ko) thio.
6. Kukur le hār khā(ko) thio.

LESSON 8

VOCABULARY

formerly—*uile, agi*
town—*sār*
regiment—*paltan*
farm (cattle)—*goth*
cowherd—*gothālā*
to be—*hunu*
to remain—*rahanu*
high hills—*lekh, himāl*
like this—*esto*
like that—*testo*
head—*tāuko*

PAST HABITUAL

I USED TO DO

In this tense we add the terminations *thien, this, thio* to the stem of the verb and not to the Past Participle as in the previous tense (the Past Perfect). Being a past tense of a transitive verb the pronoun must be in the Agent Case.

main le gar-thien—I USED TO DO
tain le gar-this—THOU USED TO DO
u le gar-thio—HE USED TO DO

NEGATIVE

The negative of this tense is irregular and very strange. We go back to the negative of the Present Habitual (See Lesson 4), *main le gardaina,* and add the terminations as in the Positive (*thien, this, thio*). Thus

main le gardaina thien—I USED NOT TO DO
tain le gardaina this—THOU USED NOT TO DO
u le gardaina thio—HE USED NOT TO DO

and so on, in the plural.

To form the above negative of verbs with a vowel before the *nu* termination, take the short negative as in the Present Habitual and add the above terminations, e.g.,

WE USED NOT TO COME—*hami āunna thio*

(The pronoun is *not* in the Agent Case as the verb is intransitive).

THEY USED NOT TO STAND HERE—*yahāṅ ubhinna thio*

HE USED NOT TO FRIGHTEN US—*hami lāi tarsāunna thio*

Remember the **Eastern** tendency to employ the long negative with these verbs: *hami āundaina thio*—WE USED NOT TO COME.

Sentences

English

1. Formerly there used not to be a railway station in this town
2. This regiment used to live in Subathu.
3. The cowherds used to remain in the farms.
4. The men used to go to the high hills on holiday.
5. He used not to shake his head like that.
6. He always used to stay at home at night.

Nepali

1. Uile yo sār māṅ tesan hunna thio.
2. Yo paltan Subāthu māṅ basthio.
3. Gothālā haru goth māṅ rahanthio.
4. Māṅchhe haru bidā māṅ lekh tira jānthio.
5. Testo / Tesori } tāuko halāunna thio.
6. U rāti sadhaiṅ ghar māṅ rahanthio (basthio).

LESSON 9

VOCABULARY

to receive, get, find, to be able (in the sense of getting an opportunity)—*pāunu*

a little—*ali, ali kati*

period, time—*kher*

a short while—*ali kher*

at what time?—*kati kher?*

to learn—*siknu*

to teach—*sikāunu*

how much? how many?—*kati, katti?*

AORIST, OR PRESENT SUBJUNCTIVE

LET ME DO ; MAY I DO

maiṅ le garuṅ—LET ME DO ; MAY I DO
taiṅ le gar—MAY THOU DO
u le garawas (or *garos*)—LET HIM DO ; MAY HE DO

In the spoken form of the language the 3rd person, *garawas* or *garos* is often employed for all persons; e.g.,

LET ME GO NOW—*Maṅ aile jānu pāwas*

NEGATIVE

maiṅ le na garuṅ—LET ME NOT DO ; MAY I NOT DO
taiṅ le na gar—MAY THOU NOT DO
u le na garawas (or *garos*)—LET HIM NOT DO ; MAY HE NOT DO

Sentences

ENGLISH

1. Let him go on leave to Nepal.
2. In order that you may learn.
3. Let them sit for a few moments.

NEPALI

1. U Gurkhā māṅ chutti (bidā) māṅ jānu pāwas.
2. Timi haru le sikos.
3. Ali kher basos (*or* basnu pāwas).

(NOTE: This construction is largely used with the *bhanera* construction, when *bhanera* is used to mean IN ORDER TO, WITH THE OBJECT OF. This will be studied in Lesson 35, para. 4.)

LESSON 10

VOCABULARY

seed—*biu*
to sow (seed)—*charnu*
to plant—*ropnu*
seedling, plant, sapling—*biruwā*
rice (growing)—*dhān*
rice (grain)—*chāṅwal*
rice (cooked)—*bhāt*
at once, immediately—*jhattā*; *chito*
to win, beat—*jitnu*
government—*sarkār*
servant—*chākar*
to look after—*herchār garnu*, *pālnu*

FUTURE

I SHALL DO

This tense has two forms in the Positive, but only one in the Negative.

POSITIVE

maṅ garne chhu—I SHALL or WILL DO
taṅ garne chhas—THOU SHALT or WILT DO
u garne chha—HE SHALL or WILL DO

POSITIVE (ALTERNATIVE FORM)

maṅ garuṅlā
taṅ garlās
u garlā

NEGATIVE

maṅ garne chhaina—I SHALL NOT or WILL NOT DO
taṅ garne chhainas—THOU SHALT NOT or WILT NO DO
u garne chhaina—HE SHALL NOT or WILL NOT DO

Remember that the Present Habitual Tense (Lesson 4) can always be used for the Near Future.

The difference in meaning of the two Positive forms, *maṅ garne chhu* and *maṅ garuṅlā* is that the latter is a little stronger, i.e., I *will* DO IT. Note also the form *gar*NU *chha*—IS TO DO IT.

The form *garne ho*—YOU WILL DO IT is really an alternative Imperative.

Sentences

ENGLISH

1. We will sow the seeds this evening.
2. We will plant the rice tomorrow.
3. We shall go on parade at once.
4. Our soldiers will beat the Japanese.
5. The Government will always look after its servants.
6. I have to go to the bazar the day after tomorrow.
7. He will go to Dehra Dun shortly.
8. He will not be frightened.

1. Hami āju beluki biu charlā.
2. Hami bholi dhān roplā.
3. Hami jhatta kawāz māṅ jālā.
4. Hamro mānchhe haru Jāpan lāi jitlā.
5. Sarkār sadhaiṅ āphnu chākar haru lāi her chār garlā.
6. Maṅ parsi pasal māṅ jānu chha.

(NOTE: The third person termination is usually used in this construction for all persons.)

7. U bholi parsi Dehra Dun māṅ jāne chha.
8. U tarsine chhaina.

LESSON 11

VOCABULARY

up to, until—*samma, sama*
many, very—*dherai*
a casualty—*ghāite*
wounded—*ghāil bhā ko*

FUTURE PERFECT

I SHALL HAVE DONE

Here we take the Past Participle *gariā ko* and add the future of the verb TO BE—*hunu*; future, *huṅlā, holās, holā*. As we are using a Past Participle we put the pronoun in the Agent Case:

maiṅ le gariā(ko) huṅlā—I SHALL HAVE DONE
taiṅ le gariā(ko) holās—THOU SHALT HAVE DONE
u le gariā(ko) holā—HE SHALL (or WILL) HAVE DONE

NEGATIVE

maiṅ le gariā(ko) hune chhaina—I SHALL NOT HAVE DONE
taiṅ le gariā(ko) hune chhainas—THOU SHALT NOT HAVE DONE
u le gariā(ko) hune chhaina—HE SHALL (or WILL) NOT HAVE DONE

Note here that the Future of the verb TO BE (*holā*) added to any tense of the verb gives the idea of doubt rendered by the English word PROBABLY:

gayo (colloquial *go*)—HE HAS GONE
gayo holā—HE HAS PROBABLY GONE
garlā—HE WILL DO IT
garlā holā—HE WILL PROBABLY DO IT
garchha—HE DOES IT
garchha holā—HE PROBABLY DOES IT

NEGATIVE

The negative is formed by putting the main verb in the negative.

gardaina holā—HE PROBABLY DOES NOT DO IT
garina holā—HE PROBABLY DID NOT DO IT
garne chhaina holā—HE PROBABLY WILL NOT DO IT

and so on.

Sentences

ENGLISH

1. We shall have marched fifteen miles by tomorrow.
2. The recruits will have arrived by this evening.
3. I shall have eaten my rations by the day after tomorrow.
4. The enemy will have had many casualties.

NEPALI

1. Bholi samma hami pandra "mile" hiṅriā(ko) holā.
2. Āju beluki samma rakrut haru āipugiā(ko) holā.
3. Mero rāsan parsi samma khā(ko) holā.
4. Bairi (dushman) ko dherai ghāite bhā(ko) holā.

LESSON 12

VOCABULARY

hither, to here—*etā, ittā, yetā*
who?—*ko*?
which?—*kun*?
place—*thāuṅ*
to kill—*mārnu, mārdinu*
to die—*marnu*
equipment—*tānā bānā*
to lose (game, competition)—*hārnu*
to lose (misplace)—*harāunu*
competition—*bāzi*

PAST CONDITIONAL

I SHOULD (WOULD) HAVE DONE

mań (or *maiń le*) *garne thień*—I SHOULD (WOULD) HAVE DONE
tań (or *taiń le*) *garne this*—THOU SHOULDST (WOULDST) HAVE DONE
u (or *u le*) *garne thio*—HE SHOULD (WOULD) HAVE DONE

NEGATIVE

mań (or *maiń le*) *garne thina*—I SHOULD (WOULD) NOT HAVE DONE
tań (or *taiń le*) *garne thinas*—THOU SHOULDST (WOULDST) NOT HAVE DONE
u (or *u le*) *garne thina*—HE SHOULD (WOULD) NOT HAVE DONE

Note the form: *gar-nu thień, this, thio* (Negative—*gar-nu thina, thinas, thina*) which means OUGHT TO HAVE DONE. Thus,

Company Commander sāhab lāi bhannu thio—HE OUGHT TO HAVE TOLD THE COMPANY COMMANDER;

but, *Company Commander sāhab lāi bhanne thio*—HE WOULD HAVE TOLD THE COMPANY COMMANDER.

The above Tense will be again used when we study the Conditional at length in Lesson 27.

Note on All Tenses Studied So Far

We observe that with the exception of the following tenses, the AORIST, the FUTURE and FUTURE PERFECT ending in *lā* and *holā* (3rd person singular), all the tenses are formed (3rd person singular), by adding either *chha* or *thio* to (i) the root, (ii) the infinitive, (iii) the inflected infinitive (*garne*), or (iv) the past participle (*gariāko*). This fact should help students when committing to memory.

Root	*gar*	
Infin.	*garnu*	add *chha* (3rd person)
Inflected Infin.	*garne*	or
		add *thio* (3rd person)
Past Participle	*gariāko*	

garchha, garthio—DOES, USED TO DO.

garnu chha, garnu thio—WILL HAVE TO DO, OUGHT TO HAVE DONE.

garne chha, garne thio—WILL DO, WOULD (SHOULD) HAVE DONE.

gariāko chha, gariāko thio—IS DOING (HAS DONE), WAS DOING (HAD DONE).

Sentences

ENGLISH

1. He should have arrived by yesterday evening.
2. We should have told the havildar.
3. You should not have come here.
4. To what place should he have gone?
5. He ought not to have gone to the bazar at night.
6. He would have killed the Jap.
7. You should not have come on parade like this.
8. He should not have lost his equipment.
9. They should not have lost the football match.

NEPALI

1. U hijo beluki samma āipugne thio.
2. Hami le havildār lāi (sita) bhannu thio.
3. Taṅ yahāṅ (yeta) āunu thinas.
4. Tio kun thāuṅ māṅ jānu thio aṅ?
5. U rāti pasal māṅ jānu thina.
6. U le Jāpan lāi mārne thio.
7. Taṅ esto (bhaera) kawāz māṅ āunu thinas.
8. U le āphnu tāna bāna harāunu thina.
9. Uni haru football ko bāzi māṅ hārne thina.
   (Note here, as *hārnu* is intransitive the pronoun is not in the AGENT CASE, and we say *bāzi māṅ*—IN THE FOOTBALL MATCH.)

LESSON 13

VOCABULARY

door (small)—*dailo*
door (large), gate—*dhokā*
to open—*ughārnu*
to be opened (intr.)—*ughrinu*
quickly—*chito, chāṅro*
to wash (body) (intr.)—*nuhāunu*
stone—*dhungā*
to put, place—*rākhnu*
to catch hold of, grab—*samātnu*
money—*paisā*
boots, shoes—*juttā*
to rub, polish—*malnu*
to be extended, to spread (intr.)—*phailinu*
to extend, spread out (tr.)—*phailāunu*
right—*dāhine*
left—*bāheṅ, debre*
now—*aile*
to show (by pointing out)—*dekhāunu*
to show (by verbal explanation)—*batāunu*

IMPERATIVE

DO, BE PLEASED TO DO, etc.

In order to form the simple Imperative DO, we cut off the final *nu* of the Infinitive of a verb, and what remains is the IMPERATIVE.

garnu—TO DO	Imp.	*gar*—DO!
basnu—TO SIT	,,	*bas*—SIT!
bolnu—TO SPEAK	,,	*bol*—SPEAK!
bhannu—TO SAY	,,	*bhan*—SAY!

Verbs ending in *inu,* all of which are intransitive, follow the above rule. Their Imperative ends, therefore, in an *i.*

halinu—TO MOVE, SHAKE	Imp.	*hali*—MOVE!
ubhinu—TO STAND	,,	*ubhi*—STAND (UP)!
tarsinu—TO FEAR	,,	*tarsi*—FEAR!

Verbs ending in *āunu* cut off the *u* as well as the *nu,* leaving a final long *ā*.

halāunu—TO SHAKE	Imp.	*halā*—SHAKE!
tarsāunu—TO FRIGHTEN	,,	*tarsā*—FRIGHTEN!
garāunu—TO CAUSE TO DO	,,	*garā*—CAUSE TO DO!

Verbs ending in *ānu* follow the general rule.

khānu—TO EAT	Imp.	*khā*—EAT!
jānu—TO GO	,,	*jā*—GO!
lānu—TO TAKE (WITH)	,,	*lā*—TAKE (WITH)!

Verbs of which the Imperative ends in a consonant such as *gar ! bas ! bol ! bhan !*, as given above, have a plural form of the Imperative usually employed when speaking to more than one person. This is formed by adding a short *a* to the form of the Imperative given above. Thus

gar becomes *gara*		*bol* becomes *bola*	
bas ,, *basa*		*bhan* ,, *bhana*	

Great care must be taken to pronounce this final *a* short and not long ; for if it is pronounced long, it will, in many cases, form the Imperative of the transitive or causative form of the same verb, the Infinitive of which ends in *āunu* (See the Imperative of verbs ending in *āunu,* explained above). For instance,

If the final short *a* in *gara* (DO! when addressing more than one person) is pronounced long *ā* it will mean CAUSE TO DO—*garā !* In the same way *sika* means LEARN! (addressing more than one person), but *sikā* means TEACH!

The use of the Infinitive of the verb as a polite Imperative is not true Nepali and is borrowed from Urdu in which it is often used ; e.g.,

Jaldi karnā (Urdu)—PLEASE BE QUICK

Chito garnu (Nepali)—PLEASE BE QUICK

If a polite form is required it is far better to use the form *garnu holā*—WILL YOU PLEASE DO, or *garnu hawas*—MAY YOU DO (3rd person). (See the AORIST TENSE, Lesson 9). With these polite forms YOU is translated by *tapāiṅ* or *āphu*, and by Thaukuris and Chettris by *hazur* with the verb in the 3rd person singular ; e.g.,

WILL YOU PLEASE SIT HERE—*Tapāiṅ yahāṅ basnu hawas* (sometimes contracted to *basnos*)

A very polite form used by juniors to people much their senior is used by Thaukuris and Chettris and is very common at the Capital. It is formed by adding the verb *baksinu*—(TO BE KIND, CHARITABLE) to the short Past Participle of the other verb.

BE KIND ENOUGH TO SPEAK—*Boli baksinu holā* (*hawas*)
BE KIND ENOUGH TO DO—*Gari baksinu holā* (*hawas*)

NOTE: *Baksinu hawas* is often contracted to *baksios*.

FORMATION OF THE NEGATIVE

The negative of all forms of the Imperative is rendered by adding the word *na* before the positive form ; e.g.,

DON'T DO—*Na gar*

DON'T SIT THERE, YOU MEN (plural)—*Tahāṅ na basa*

DON'T PLEASE COME TOMORROW—*Tapāiṅ bholi na āunu holā* (*hawas*)

FUTURE IMPERATIVE

A common form not found in Urdu is that of the Future Imperative. It is used when an action is described as taking place after another action ; that is, two actions being ordered in the Imperative, the two clauses in English being joined by the word AND. It is constructed by adding *es* to the stem of the verb ; e.g.,

Basnu (stem *bas*)	Fut. Imp.	*bases*
garnu (stem *gar*)	,,	*gares*
halāunu (stem *halā*)	,,	*halāes*

Example: COME HERE AND SIT DOWN—*Yahāṅ āera bases*
GET UP QUICKLY TOMORROW MORNING AND COME TO ME—*Bholi bihāno jhatta utera maṅ sita āes*
HAVING COME HERE THIS EVENING, DON'T MAKE A NOISE—*Āju beluki yahāṅ āera khalbal na gares*

The use of this Future Imperative is peremptory and is therefore only used when speaking to an inferior or inferiors. Note that when we have two clauses in English joined by the word AND, in Nepali the first clause is usually put in the Past Participle. This applies not only to the Imperative but to all tenses.

GO TO THE OFFICE AND TELL THE CLERK TO COME HERE
is rendered
Having gone to the office, tell the clerk to come here

HE SAT ON THE FLOOR AND COUNTED HIS MONEY
is similarly rendered
Having sat on the floor, he counted his money

As to the Past Participle see Lesson 15.

Sentences

English

1. Open the door.
2. Wash quickly in the river.
3. Put those stones down quickly, you men.
4. Catch hold of that Jap and bring him here.
5. Don't bunch together.
6. Extend to the right and left.
7. Polish your boots now (Addressing more than one man).
8. Stand on the top of that hill.
9. Please come to my room quickly.
10. Please show me the road.
11. Please don't shake that tree.
12. Have the kindness to give this money to the servant.
13. Have the kindness not to tell him.

Nepali

1. Dailo ughār.
2. Kholā māṅ chito (chāṅrai) nuhā.
3. Tio dhungā haru chito rākha ai.

(Note the sound *ai* (short *a*) used after the Imperative when speaking to either one or more men. It has the effect of making the Imperative stronger. For correct pronunciation of this sound see end of Lesson 3.)

4. Tio Jāpan lāi samātera yahāṅ liera āes.
5. Na thupri ai!
6. Dahine bāheṅ phaili ai!
7. Juttā (boot) aile mala ai.
8. Tio dāṅrā māṅthi ubhi.
9. Tapāiṅ mero kothā māṅ chito āunu hawas (āunos).
10. Bāto dekhāunu holā.
11. Tio rukh na halāunu holā.
12. Chākar lāi yo paisā di baksios (baksinu hawas).
13. Hazur, u lāi na bhani baksios.

LESSON 14

Revision of Lesson 13 (the Imperative). Students to make up sentences on the Imperative.

LESSON 15

VOCABULARY

inside—*bhitra*
outside—*bāira*
to enter—*pasnu*
to swim—*paurnu* ; *pauri khelnu*
limb (arm)—*bāhāṅ*
to stretch, pull—*tānnu*
to consider, ponder—*thānnu*
war—*dhāuwa, larāi*
to fit, resemble—*milnu*
noise—*khalbal*
must—*parchha* (with infin.)
to give—*dinu* (*lāi*)
information—*tāhā*
to inform—*tāhā dinu*
tent—*pāl*
in front of, before—*agāri, aghi*
behind—*pachāri, pachi*
you must do (habitual)—*timi garnu parchha*
just—*bharkar*
to finish—*sidāunu*
to be finished—*sidinu*

PARTICIPLES

The Present and Past Participles in this language have far wider uses than in Urdu. If this lesson is mastered, a student's power of speech should greatly improve.

PRESENT PARTICIPLES

Gardā, gardo, gardā kheri, garne belā māṅ

gardā, gardo—DOING, or WHILE DOING

(More will be said of *gardo* when we come to the Conditional)

gardā kheri really means AT THE TIME OF DOING

kheri or *kher*—TIME

kati (*katti*) *kher*?—AT WHAT TIME?

uti (*utti*) *kher*—AT THAT TIME (juncture)

ali kher pachi—A SHORT TIME AFTERWARDS

ani kheri—AND THEN, (the next moment)

Garne belā māṅ also really means AT THE TIME OF, the word *belā* meaning TIME

U kun belā āunchha—AT WHAT TIME WILL HE COME?

(*āunchha,* Present Habitual used in the sense of Near Future. See Lesson 4)

WHILE is rendered *gardā gardai*—WHILE DOING

āundā āundai—WHILE COMING

PAST PARTICIPLES

Gar-era, gari, garikana, gariāko—HAVING DONE

All of these mean the same, i.e., HAVING DONE. The second form, *gari* is not used much in speaking except when it forms part of a composite verb (See Lesson 24, para. ii). It is, however, used more than any other form in writing. The form *gariāko* is used to form the past tenses of the verb ; the word *ko* usually being left out when speaking by men from Central and Western Nepal. It is also used like an adjective:

THE GOOD MEN—*rāmro mānchhe haru*

THE TALL MEN—*algo mānchhe haru*

THE FROM DEHRA DUN COMING MEN i.e. (THE MEN "WHO" ARE COMING FROM DEHRA DUN)—*Dehra Dun bāti āko mānchhe haru*

The Past participles of verbs ending in *āunu* are formed as follows:

garāunu—*garāera, garāi, garāikana, garāko*

sikāunu—*sikāera, sikāi, sikāikana, sikāko*

The use of the inflected Infinitive of a verb instead of the Past Participle gives the idea of either the Present habitual or immediate Future.

Example: THE MEN WHO ARE COMING FROM DEHRA DUN—*Dehra Dun bāti āko* (non-habitual Present) *mānchhe haru,* and

THE MEN WHO HAVE COME FROM DEHRA DUN—*Dehra Dun bāti āko mānchhe haru*, but

THE MEN WHO COME (habitually) FROM DEHRA DUN—*Dehra Dun bāti "āune" mānchhe haru*, and

THE MEN WHO WILL COME (ARE COMING, near future) FROM DEHRA DUN—*Dehra Dun bāti "āune" mānchhe haru*

The rule is, use the inflected Infinitive for the Present habitual and near future ; use the Past participle (*āko*) for the Present non-habitual and recent past.

NEGATIVE

To form the negative of any participle, Present or Past, insert ***na*** before the Positive form.

PRESENT PARTICIPLE

na gardā, na gardo, na gardā kheri, na garne belā mān

The above negative, ***na gardā,*** often in speech put in its strong form ***na gardai,*** gives the meaning of BEFORE.

HE CAME HERE BEFORE EATING HIS FOOD—*U na khāndai āyo*

PAST PARTICIPLE

The negative Past participle is sometimes used to obtain the same meaning;

u na khāikana āyo

Sentences

ENGLISH

1. He came into the room and sat on the bed.
2. While standing on the wall he over-balanced and fell.
3. Do not make a noise while I am speaking.
4. While going to his home he died.
5. In swimming you must stretch your limbs.
6. Having thought over this matter inform me tomorrow.
7. The men who are going to Nepal are in this tent.
8. The recruits who are sitting outside have just arrived.
9. The people who live in Dehra Dun are Hindus (habitual).
10. The soldiers who will sit here tomorrow.
11. When you have finished your work go to bed.
12. The men who have not done the work will come here.
13. The men who do not live in Nepal.
14. We will advance after taking that hill.
15. The men who have returned from the war will go on a month's leave.

1. Kothā bhitra pasera khāt māṅ basio.
2. Bhittā (parkhāl) māṅthi ubhindā (kheri) paltera jhario.
3. Maṅ bolne belā māṅ khalbal na gara ai.
4. Āphnu ghár māṅ jāndā jāndai mario.
(Note here, the Present participle followed by a repetition of the Present participle in its strong form. This gives the idea of continued action.)
5. Pauri kheldā kheri (māṅ) bāhāṅ tānnu parchha.
6. Yo kurā thānera maṅ lāi bholi tāhā dinu holā (polite).
7. Nepāl māṅ jāne mānchhe haru yo pāl māṅ basiā(ko) chha (chha).
8. Bāira basiāko rakrut haru bharkar āipugiā(ko)chha.
(NOTE: In using the Past participle, *gariāko, basiāko* as an adjective in this way, the *ko* is always retained both in the *Western* and *Eastern* forms of speech.)
9. Dehra Dun māṅ basne mānchhe Hindu ho (hunchha).
10. Bholi yahāṅ basne mānchhe haru (near future).
11. Kām sidāera sutes (Future Imperative).
12. Kām na gariāko mānchhe haru yahāṅ āulā.
13. Gurkhā māṅ na basne mānchhe haru (habitual).
14. Tio dāṅrā likana hami agāri barhlā (advance holā).
15. Dhāuwa māṅ gaera āko mānchhe haru ek mahina ko bidā māṅ jālā. (pāulā—WILL GET)
(Note here the use of *pāunu*—TO GET, and not *milnu*.)

LESSON 16

VOCABULARY

ill—*birāmi*
temple—*deota thān*
of the hills—*pahāri*
intelligent—*chaṅkhie, bātho*
country—*des*
woman—*āimāi, swāsni*
big—*thulo*
all—*sabai, jammai*
parade ground—*tunikhel*
this side of (linear)—*wāri*
the far side of (linear)—*pāri*
village—*gāuṅ*

CONJUGATION OF THE VERB : hunu—TO BE

Although in the verb *garnu* (TO DO), as studied above, we have employed various parts of the verb TO BE in the terminations, it is important to again study this verb carefully as it is an integral part of all other verbs. It is, moreover, irregular in its root or stem which changes in the past tenses. This lesson is devoted to the study of the Present tense of this verb, which has three forms, as below:

PRESENT TENSE

I	II	III
maṅ huṅ	*hunchhu*	*chhu*
taṅ hos	*hunchhas*	*chhas*
u or *tio ho*	*hunchha*	*chha*

NEGATIVE

Maṅ hoina	*hunna*	*chhaina*
taṅ hoinas	*hunnas*	*chhainas*
u or *tio hoina*	*hunna*	*chhaina*

The above three columns give three forms of the Present tense of the verb *hunu*—TO BE in the positive and the negative. It is most important that a student should understand how to use them.

COL. I: (3rd person singular—*ho ;* Negative—*hoina.*)

This is used when an unalterable fact is being expressed, when the verb comes after a noun.

THIS IS A HOSPITAL—*Yo hospitāl ho.*

The sentence expresses an unchangeable fact, and "hospital" being a noun, the verb follows a noun. *ho* also means YES.

COL. II: (3rd person singular—*hunchha* ; Negative—*hunna.*)

This is also used when an unalterable fact is being expressed but in this case when the verb follows any word except a noun ; i.e. adjective, preposition, adverbs, etc.

HE IS ALWAYS IN HOSPITAL—*U sadhaiṅ hospitāl māṅ hunchha*

The above sentence expresses an unchangeable fact, and the verb comes after the preposition *māṅ*.

GURKHAS ARE STRONG—*Gurkhāli (haru) balio hunchha*

This form of the verb TO BE also means BECOMES

HE BECOMES ILL—*U birāmi hunchha*

COL. III: This is used in all cases not covered by Cols. I and II ; that is, when the fact being expressed is *not* unalterable or unchangeable:

HE IS ILL—*U birāmi chha (bhaio)*

It is, moreover, used of locality when an unchangeable fact is *not* being stated.

RIFLEMAN DALBAHADUR IS NOT IN THE TENT —*Rifleman Dalbahadur pāl māṅ chhaina*

It is also used in sentences expressing possession:

HE HAS THREE SONS—*Usko tinota chorā chha*

But, I AM HIS SON—*Maṅ usko choro huṅ* (unchangeable after a noun)

Lastly, it is used in the sense of EXISTS, though Col. II, ***hunchha***, is often used.

THERE ARE FIVE RIVERS IN THE PUNJAB. (Five rivers exist, etc.)—*Punjāb māṅ pānchotā kholā chha*

Sentences

English

1. The men who are working in the fields are Gurkhas.
2. Nowadays this is not a hospital but an hotel.
3. I am a man of the hills (Hillman).
4. Are you a soldier?
5. If you drink this water you will become ill.
6. These men are very intelligent.
7. The women of this country are pretty.
8. He has a large house in Batoli.
9. All the soldiers are on the parade-ground.
10. There are two cinemas in this bazar.
11. Gurkhas are in Nepal.
12. The village is on the far side of the river.
13. The temple is on the hill (Permanently).

Nepali

1. Bāri māṅ kām gariā(ko) mānchhe haru Gurkhāli hunchha. (*Gurkhāli* is an adjective and therefore ***hunchha*** is correct, but we often find it treated as a noun—*Gurkhāli ho.*). The above sentence with *hunchha* might mean WILL BECOME GURKHAS (in the near future, using the Present habitual tense as the near future).
2. Hijo āju yo hospitāl hoina tara hotel ho.
3. Maṅ pahāri mānchhe huṅ.
4. Taṅ sipāhi hos ki?
5. Yo pāni khāera birāmi hunchhas (immediate future).
6. Yo (ini) mānchhe haru dherai chaṅkie hunchha.
7. Yo des ko āimāi haru ramro hunchha.
8. Batoli māṅ usko yotā thulo ghar chha.

9. Sabai sipāhi haru tunikhel (pared) māṅ chha.
10. Yo pasal māṅ duita senima hunchha.
11. Gurkhāli Nepāl māṅ hunchha.
12. Gāuṅ kholā pāri hunchha.
13. Deota thān daṅrā māṅ hunchha.

LESSON 17

VOCABULARY

to pitch a tent—*pāl tāngnu*
plain, open country—*phāṅt, chāur*
flat, flat country—*samma*
halting place—*bās*
to halt the night—*bās basnu*
still, yet—*ajhai* (verb in pos.)
not yet—*ajhai* (verb in neg.)
to cook—*pakāunu*
enemy—*bairi, dushman*

THE *rai-chha* CONSTRUCTION

This is the alternative form of the Present tense of any verb, formed by using the word *raichha,* which is in itself an alternative of the Present tense of the verb TO BE, with the Past particle, *gariāko,* of any other verb.

Chha, by itself, means IS, and *rai-chha* means the same thing when the speaker is making a statement containing facts or information which he himself has ascertained from enquiry or observation, etc. It therefore contains an element of surprise.

U jangal māṅ chha—HE IS IN THE JUNGLE
U jangal māṅ raichha—(I hear) HE IS IN THE JUNGLE
U le gariā(ko) raichha—(I am told) HE IS DOING IT
(Non habitual Present)

If we use the Inflected Infinitive of the verb with *raichha* we express the "habitual action" or "immediate future" sense.

U garne raichha—HE DOES IT (habitually)
U bholi garne raichha—HE IS DOING IT TO-MORROW
U hune raichha—HE IS (habitually)

NOTE: An alternative "habitual" form exists at the Capital and is common in Eastern Nepal: *Gardā ra-chha* in place of *Garne raichha.*

We therefore have the rule:

Past participle with *raichha*—Present (non-habitual) or immediate Past.

Inflected Infinitive with *raichha*—Habitual Present or immediate Future.

The negative of the "non-habitual" Present or immediate Past form, *gariā ko raichha*, is constructed by placing *na* between the *rai* and the *chha*, e.g., *U rainachha*.

HE HAS DONE—*Gariā(ko) raichha*

HE HAS NOT DONE—*Gariā(ko) rainachha*

(The form, *na gariā(ko) raichha* is used, but is not general.)

To form the negative of the habitual Present or immediate Future form, *garne raichha*, insert *na* before the *garne*; i.e. *na garne raichha*, or insert *na* between the *rai* and the *chha* as for the "non-habitual" form; i.e. *garne rainachha*. Of the two forms the first, *na garne raichha* is recommended.

NOTE: The above construction must on no account be confused with the formation of composite verbs with *rahanu*—TO REMAIN, giving the idea of continuous action. (See Lesson 24, para. 2).

Basi rahanu—TO CONTINUE SITTING

gari rahanu—TO CONTINUE DOING

boli rahanu—TO CONTINUE SPEAKING

It has no connection with this construction.

Sentences

ENGLISH

1. The company is in camp in the jungle on the far side of the river (it appears).
2. The Japs are advancing towards the village (I am told).
3. The soldiers are now in the open plain.
4. The recruits from Dehra Dun have arrived.
5. The Gurkhas are not staying the night in Lahore.
6. The Japs are not now in Rangoon.
7. The men have not yet cooked their food.
8. Jemadar Manbir's sons live in Dehra Dun.
9. He comes here every day.
10. This man does not speak (habitually).
11. There is no bazar in this village.

NEPALI

1. Kampani pāl tāngera kholā pāri jangal māṅ basiā(ko) raichha.
2. Jāpan haru gāuṅ tira barhiā(ko) raichha.
3. Sipāhi haru aile phāṅt māṅ raichha.
4. Dehra Dun bāti āko rakrut haru āipugiā(ko) raichha.

5. Gurkhāli haru Lahore māṅ bās basiā(ko) rainachha.
6. Rangoon māṅ aile Jāpan haru rainachha.
7. Mānchhe haru le ajhai bhāt pakā rainachhā.
8. Jamdār Manbir ko chorā haru Dehra Dun māṅ basne raichha.
9. U dine piche yahāṅ āune raichha.
10. Yo mānchhe na bolne raichha.
11. Yo gāuṅ māṅ pasal na hune raichha (hune rainachha).

LESSON 18

VOCABULARY

person—*janā*
last year—*por, por sāl*
but—*tara*
the one—*chaiṅ, chāine*
ever—*kaile pani* (verb in pos.)
never—*kaile pani* (verb in neg.)
jail—*jhel khāna*
recruit—*rakrut*

So far only the Present Tense of *hunu*—TO BE has been dealt with.

IMPERFECT

I WAS

Maṅ thieṅ—I WAS
taṅ this—THOU WAST
u thio—HE WAS

NEGATIVE

Maṅ thina—I WAS NOT
taṅ thinas—THOU WAST NOT
u thina—HE WAS NOT

PAST INDICATIVE

I WAS, or BECAME

NOTE: In all Past tenses where the root is *bhā*, in addition to the meaning of WAS, HAS BEEN, HAD BEEN, etc., the meaning BECAME, HAS BECOME, HAD BECOME, etc., is rendered.

Maṅ bhaeṅ—I WAS or BECAME
taṅ bhais—THOU WAST or BECAMEST
u bhaio (*bho*)—HE WAS or BECAME

NEGATIVE

Man bhaina—I WAS NOT or DID NOT BECOME
tan bhainas—THOU WAST NOT or DIDST NOT BECOME
u bhaina—HE WAS NOT or DID NOT BECOME

PERFECT

I HAVE BEEN, or HAVE BECOME

Man bhā(ko) chhu—I HAVE BEEN or HAVE BECOME
tan bhā(ko) chhas—THOU HAST BEEN or HAST BECOME
u bhā(ko) chha (colloquial form, *bhai chha*)—HE HAS BEEN or HAS BECOME

NEGATIVE

Man bhā(ko) chhaina—I HAVE NOT BEEN or BECOME
tan bhā(ko) chhainas—THOU HAST NOT BEEN or BECOME
u bhā(ko) chhaina—HE HAST NOT BEEN or BECOME

Sentences

ENGLISH

1. Five men were in the field.
2. Last year you were not in our regiment.
3. He arrived from leave and became ill.
4. The father was a Subadar but the son did not become one.
5. He has been ill five times.
6. He has never been in jail.
7. The recruits who are not ill must come here.

NEPALI

1. Pānch janā mānchhe bāri mān thio.
2. Por tan hamro paltan mān thinas.
3. Bidā bāti āera (āipugera) birāmi bho.
4. Bābu Subadār thio tara choro chain subadār bhaina.
5. U pānch pāli birāmi bhā(ko) chha.
6. U kaile pani jhel khāna mān bhā(ko) chhaina.
7. Birāmi na bhāko rakrut haru etā āunu parchha. (See Lesson 15 for use of the Past participle in this way.)

LESSON 19

VOCABULARY

trouble—*dukha*
marriage—*bihā*
cold weather—*hiundo*
elder brother—*dāju*
riches—*dhan*
rich—*dhani*
comfort—*sancha, sukha*
younger brother—*bhāi*

PAST PERFECT

I HAD BEEN OR BECOME

Maṅ bhā(ko) thieṅ—I HAD BEEN OR BECOME
taṅ bhā(ko) this—THOU HADST BEEN OR BECOME
u bhā(ko) thio—HE HAD BEEN OR BECOME

NEGATIVE

Maṅ bhā(ko) thina—I HAD NOT BEEN OR BECOME
taṅ bhā(ko) thinas—THOU HADST NOT BEEN OR BECOME
u bhā(ko) thina—HE HAD NOT BEEN OR BECOME

PAST HABITUAL

I USED TO BE

Maṅ hunthieṅ—I USED TO BE
taṅ hunthis—THOU USED TO BE
u hunthio—HE USED TO BE

NEGATIVE

Maṅ hunna (hundaina) thieṅ—I USED NOT TO BE
taṅ hunna (hundaina) this—THOU USED NOT TO BE
u hunna (hundaina) thio—HE USED NOT TO BE

AORIST, OR PRESENT SUBJUNCTIVE

LET ME BE, MAY I BE

Maṅ huṅ—LET ME BE, MAY I BE
taṅ ho—LET THOU BE, MAY THOU BE
u hawas (hos)—LET HIM BE, MAY HE BE

NEGATIVE

Maṅ na huṅ—MAY I NOT BE
taṅ na ho—MAY THOU NOT BE
u na hawas—MAY HE NOT BE

Sentences

ENGLISH

1. He had been in trouble.
2. His marriage had taken place (had been) in the cold weather.
3. His father had been very rich.
4. Formerly there used to be a temple on the hill.
5. There used not to be a gate here.
6. May he get well quickly.
7. When his younger brother arrives do not let the dog be in the house.

NEPALI

1. U dukha māṅ bhā(ko) thio [Usko dukha bhā(ko) thio].
2. Usko bihā hiuṅdo māṅ bhā(ko) thio.
3. Usko bābu dherai dhani bhā(ko) thio.
4. Uile uile dāṅrā māṅ deota thān hunthio.
5. Dhokā yahāṅ hunna thio.
   (NOTE: LARGE GATE—*dhokā ;* SMALL DOOR—*dailo.*)
6. U lāi chito sancha hawas.
7. Usko bhāi āipugdā kheri kukur ghar bhitra na hawas.

LESSON 20

VOCABULARY

to spend (money)—*māsnu* poor—*kaṅgāli*

FUTURE

I SHALL BE

As shewn in Lesson 10 this tense has two forms in the Positive but only one in the Negative.

POSITIVE

Maṅ hune chhu—I SHALL OF WILL BE
taṅ hune chhas—THOU SHALT OF WILT BE
u hune chha—HE SHALL OF WILL BE

ALTERNATIVE FORM OF POSITIVE

Maṅ huṅlā
taṅ holās
u holā

NEGATIVE

Maṅ hune chhaina
taṅ hune chhainas
u hune chhaina

FUTURE PERFECT

I SHALL HAVE BEEN OF BECOME

Maṅ bhā(ko) huṅlā—I SHALL HAVE BEEN
taṅ bhā(ko) holās—THOU SHALT HAVE BEEN
u bhā(ko) holā—HE SHALL HAVE BEEN

NEGATIVE

Maṅ bhā(ko) hune chhaina—I SHALL NOT HAVE BEEN or BECOME

taṅ bhā(ko) hune chhainas—THOU SHALT NOT HAVE BEEN or BECOME

u bhā(ko) hune chhaina—HE SHALL NOT HAVE BEEN or BECOME

Sentences

ENGLISH

1. We will be on that hill in ten minutes.
2. Having drunk this he will be strong.
3. Not having run (unless you run) you will be late.
4. Having spent your money you will be poor.
5. Having not washed (if he does not wash) he will be ill.
6. When my father comes here I shall not have become a Jamadar.

NEPALI

1. Hami das minit samma tio dāṅrā māṅ holā.
2. Yo khāera balio holā (hune chha).
3. Na dugrera abelā hune chhas. (Note here the tendency in this language to omit the pronoun.)
4. Āphnu paisā māsera kaṅgāli holās.
5. Na nuhāera birāmi holā.
6. Mero bābu yahāṅ āune belā māṅ maṅ Jemadar bhā(ko) hune chhaina.

LESSON 21

VOCABULARY

happy—*ramāilo* unhappy—*naramāilo* to be happy—*ramāunu*

PAST CONDITIONAL

I SHOULD or WOULD HAVE BEEN

Maṅ hune thieṅ—I SHOULD or WOULD HAVE BEEN

taṅ hune this—THOU SHOULDST or WOULDST HAVE BEEN

u hune thio—HE SHOULD or WOULD HAVE BEEN

NEGATIVE

Maṅ hune thina—I SHOULD or WOULD NOT HAVE BEEN
taṅ hune thinas—THOU SHOULDST or WOULDST NOT HAVE BEEN
u hune thina—HE SHOULD or WOULD NOT HAVE BEEN

Note the form *hunu thio*, (Neg. *hunu thina*) meaning SHOULD or OUGHT TO HAVE BEEN.

IMPERATIVE

Ho—BE!

Hunu holā, or *hunu hawas* (polite form)—PLEASE BE!
Hoi baksios, or *hoi baksinu holā* (super polite. See Lesson 13).

NEGATIVE

na ho, na hunu holā, na hunu hawas, na hoi baksios, etc.

Sentences

ENGLISH

1. He should have been here when I came.
2. He ought to have been in his house.
3. You should not have been on the parade.
4. They would have been ill.
5. You (people) would have been rich
6. Please don't be unhappy.

NEPALI

1. Maṅ āundā kheri u yahāṅ hune thio.
2. U āphnu ghar māṅ hunu thio.
3. Taṅ kawāz māṅ hunu thinas.
4. Uni haru birāmi hune thio.
5. Timi haru dhani hune thio.
6. Naramāilo na hunu hawas.
   (Note the form *na hawas*. This is not so polite as *na hunu hawas*.)

LESSON 22

VOCABULARY

water—*pāni*
cold (of weather)—*jāro*
wet, cold (of water)—*chiso*
sadness—*surtā*
warm—*garam*
hot (of water)—*tāto*
to be sad—*surtā lāgnu* (*lāi*)

PARTICIPLES

Present Participles: *hundā, hundo, hundā kheri, hune belā māṅ*

Past Participles: *hoi, bhai, bha-era, bhai-kana, bhāko* (used like an adjective)

These participles are used exactly as explained in Lesson 15. Remember the tendency to put the first clause in the Past participle, where in English two clauses are joined by "and", e.g.,

HE WAS ILL AND LAY DOWN—*Birāmi bhaera sutio*

Remember also the use of the inflected Infinitive like an adjective in the relative sense where the Present habitual or near Future is implied, and the Past participle *bhāko* (*ko* cannot be left out), when non-habitual Present or recent Past is implied, e.g.,

Dhani hune mānchhe—MEN WHO GET RICH (habitual)

But, *Dhani bhāko mānchhe*—THE MAN WHO IS GETTING (BECOMING) RICH, or HAS BECOME RICH

The form, *hundo*—BEING, is not much used, its employment being most frequent in Conditional tenses explained in Lesson 27.

Sentences

ENGLISH

1. When in the water it is cold.
2. You must come when I am in the tent.
3. When my son is not here I am sad.
4. The men who are in Dehra Dun.
5. The Japanese who are across the river.
6. Before being married he died.
7. Having been enlisted he came to Dehra Dun.

NEPALI

1. Pāni māṅ hundā kheri jāro hunchha.
   (NOTE: THE WATER IS COLD—*Pāni chiso chha.*)
2. Maṅ pāl māṅ hundā kheri timi āunu parchha.
3. Mero choro yahāṅ na hune belā māṅ maṅ lāi ta surtā lāgchha.
4. Dehra Dun māṅ hune mānchhe haru.
5. Kholā pāri bhāko Jāpan haru.
6. Bihā na hundai mario.
7. Bharti bhaikana Dehra Dun māṅ āyo.

LESSON 23

THE POLITE FORM OF THE VERB

Every verb in the language, including the verb TO BE—*hunu,* has a polite form. It is used when speaking not only *to* a superior but also *of* a superior even if the superior is not present. Its use in the polite Imperative, *garnu holā* or *garnu hawas,* is commonly known by students ; its other tenses, especially when used in speaking of a superior when he is not present, being often ignored. This is not surprising as uneducated Gurkhas very often themselves ignore it when speaking *of* a superior but not when speaking *to* a superior.

CONSTRUCTION OF POLITE FORM

The polite form may be constructed in any tense by adding to the Infinitive of the verb the appropriate tense of the verb *hunu*—TO BE, e.g.,

THE GENERAL SAHAB IS SITTING HERE—*General Sāhab yahāṅ basnu bhā(ko) chha*

WHAT DID THE COMPANY COMMANDER SAHAB SAY?—*Company Commander Sāhab le ke bhannu bhā(ko) thio*

THE COLONEL SAHAB IS NOT IN HIS TENT—*Colonel Sāhab āphnu pāl māṅ hunu hunna*

Note here the form *hunu hunna. Hunu bhāko chhaina* would mean HAS NOT BECOME, in the polite form.

In Lesson 13 we described a super-polite form used by Thaukuris and Chettris with the verb *baksinu*—TO BE KIND, CHARITABLE. This may be used in any tense by adding the polite form of *baksinu* to the short Past Participle of the main verb, e.g.,

HAVE THE HONOUR TO SIT HERE—*Yahāṅ basi baksinu hawas* (contracted to *baksios*)

THE COLONEL SAHAB IS PLAYING FOOTBALL—*Colonel Sāhab le foot-ball kheli baksinu bhā(ko) chha*

THE COMPANY COMMANDER IS NOT HERE—*Company Commander Sāhab yahāṅ hoi baksinu hunna*

NOTE: It is, however, quite out of place for Officers to use this construction even to Gurkha officers. It should, however, be known.

Sentences

ENGLISH

1. Have you had your food? (Speaking to a superior).
2. The company commander has told him.
3. The General was (became) ill.
4. Please don't go into the house.
5. When will you play football? (Polite form)
6. The Sahab has not come on parade.
7. The Colonel Sahab is going to Dehra Dun tomorrow.

NEPALI

1. Tapāiṅ le khānu bho?
2. Company Commander Sāhab le u lāi bhannu bho.
3. General Sāhab birāmi hunu bhaio (bho); or "hunu bhā(ko) thio."
4. Ghar māṅ na pasnu holā.
5. Tapāiṅ (Āphu) kaile "football" khelnu hunchha? (Immediate future).
6. Sāhab pared (kawāz) māṅ āunu bhā chhaina.

   (NOTE: In Nepal, when using the polite form of TO COME or TO GO, the verb *pālnu* is often used: THE GENERAL SAHAB HAS NOT COME—*General Sāhab pālnu bhā(ko) chhaina* etc.)
7. Colonel Sāhab bholi Dehra Dun māṅ pālnu hunchha.

LESSON 24

COMPOUND VERBS

In the Nepali language the employment of Compound verbs—that is, two verbs joined together to obtain a certain meaning—is very common, especially in speech. Most of them are formed by adding a verb to either the short Past participle or to the stem of another verb. (Short Past participle of *garnu*—*gari*. Stem—*gar*.)

In our use of the verb *baksinu* in the previous lesson, we have already learnt one compound verb formed by adding *baksinu* to the short Past participle of another verb to give the meaning of TO BE KIND ENOUGH TO DO ANYTHING. Other examples are:

1. The adding of any tense of the verb *dinu*—TO GIVE to the stem of any transitive verb, except when added to verbs ending in *āunu*, when it is added to the Past Participle *āi*, (e.g., *garāi dinu*). This has the effect of emphasising or strengthening the first verb, and is very common in speech, especially in the Imperative.

gar—DO! but *garde*—DO IT THEN!

YOU MUST BEAT THAT DOG—*Tio kukur (lāi) hāndinu parchha*

HE HAS TOLD HIM—*U lāi bhandiā(ko) chha*
(colloquial—*bhandi chha*)

NOTE: If we add *dinu* to the Infinitive of a verb we get the meaning of TO ALLOW:

HE HAS ALLOWED HIM TO SIT—*Basnu dio (diā ko chha)*

2. The adding of the verb *rahanu*—TO REMAIN to the short Past participle of any verb to express continuous action. This form is very common in speech and is often used in cases where the action is not really continuous but of short duration. It is also the best form to use when expressing the non-habitual Present tense:

THEY ARE SITTING INSIDE THE ROOM—*Uni haru kothā bhitra basi rahā chha*

But, THEY CONTINUALLY GO TO DEHRA DUN—*Uni haru Dehra Dun māṅ gai rahanchha* (habitual)

HE HAD LIVED IN NEPAL FOR THREE YEARS—*U tin sāl (barkha) samma Gurkhā māṅ basi rahā(ko) thio*

WHY ARE YOU ALL TALKING (SPEAKING)?—*Timi haru sabai janā kina boli rahā chha*

NOTE: It is important not to confuse the above construction with the *raichha* construction explained in LESSON 17, with which it has no connection.

3. The use of the verb *saknu* after the short Past participle of another verb to give the meaning of COMPLETING OF FINISHING:

HE HAS FINISHED THE WORK—*U le kām gari sakio*

Bihāunu also means TO FINISH:

MY WORK WILL NOT BE FINISHED TODAY—*Āju mero kām bihāunna*

It is also used in the sense of TO HAVE TIME:

HAVE YOU TIME TO DO IT NOW?—*Aile timi lāi bihāunchha ki bihāunna* (Eastern: *bihāundaina*)

The verb *saknu* when used with the Infinitive of the other verb means TO BE ABLE in all senses except in the sense of getting an opportunity, or permission, when *pāunu* must always be used. *Pāunu* also means TO FIND or TO GET. In the sense of mental ability use *jānnu*:

HE CANNOT READ—*U parnu jāndaina*

HE IS UNABLE TO WALK—*U hiṅrnu sakdaina*, but

HE IS UNABLE TO GO TO DEHRA DUN (no opportunity)—*U Dehra Dun māṅ jānu pāunna* (Eastern: *pāundaina*)

MAY WE SMOKE?—*Hami "cigarette" khānu pāunchha ki?*
(*pāunchha ki pāunna*)

YOU CAN GET POTATOES IN THE BAZAR—*Pasal māṅ ālu pāunchha*
(*milnu* means TO FIT, and should not be used)

NOTE: The use of *pathāunu*—TO SEND, when used with the Infinitive of another verb, means TO CAUSE:

HE MADE THEM (CAUSED THEM TO) SIT—*Ue le uni haru lāi basnu pathāio*.

Māngnu—TO DEMAND, ASK FOR *Mangāunu*—TO SEND FOR

Mangāi pathāunu—TO CAUSE TO BE SENT FOR (of inanimate objects)

Bolāi pathāunu—TO SUMMON (of human beings)

Dehra Dun bāti ālu mangāi pathāunu parchha—WE MUST SEND TO DEHRA DUN FOR POTATOES

Note also the use of the verb *hālnu*—TO PUT IN, to render the idea of FINISHING OFF:

Gari hālio—HE HAS ALREADY DONE IT (finished it)

U lāi bhani hāliā(ko) chha—HE HAS ALREADY TOLD HIM

Gari hāl !—FINISH IT OFF!

The use of the verb *rākhnu*—TO PLACE, PUT, with the short Past participle of a transitive verb renders the meaning of BEFORE or BEFOREHAND or TO PLACE PERMANENTLY:

Uni haru lāi bhani rākh !—WARN THEM!

Yo postok kotal gād māṅ di rākh—GIVE THIS BOOK INTO THE QUARTER GUARD (literally: GIVE AND PLACE)

LESSON 25

VOCABULARY

trousers—*suruāl*

to apply, wear—*lāunu*

to hunt (animals or birds)—*shikār khelnu*

SENTENCES INTRODUCING USE OF COMPOUND VERBS

1. THE GENERAL SAHAB WAS KIND ENOUGH TO GIVE HIM RS. 10/-.
General Sāhab le u lāi das rupiā di baksinu bho.
2. HAVE THE HONOUR TO ALLOW HIM TO SPEAK.
U lāi bolnu di baksinu holā (baksios).
3. GIVE ALL THE RIFLES TO THE RECRUITS.
Sabai rifle haru rakrut haru lāi dide.
4. YOU MUST TELL HIM TOMORROW MORNING.
U lāi bholi bihāno bhandinu parchha.

5. WHY ARE THOSE MEN WEARING TROUSERS?
Tio (uni) mānchhe haru le kina suruāl lāi rahā (ko) chha?

6. HOW MANY TIMES HAVE I GOT TO TELL YOU?
Timi haru lāi kati pālī bhani rahanu parchha?

7. THE MEN ARE ALL BUNCHING.
Mānchhe haru sabai (jammai) thupri rahā (ko) chha.

8. HE HAS ALREADY TOLD HIM (HE HAS FINISHED TELLING HIM).
U lāi bhani sakiā (ko) chha.

NOTE: TO FINISH, when not used with another verb, use *sidinu* (intr.) *sidāunu* (trans.).

HE HAS FINISHED HIS WORK—*Āphnu kām sidāio*

HIS WORK IS FINISHED—*Usko kām sidio*

I HAVE FINISHED WHAT I HAVE TO SAY—*Mero kurā sidio*

9. THEY HAVE ALREADY HAD THEIR FOOD.
Uni haru (le) khāi hāliā (ko) chha.

10. I AM UNABLE TO TELL YOU.
Maṅ timi lāi bhannu sakdaina.

11. I AM FORBIDDEN TO TELL YOU.
Maṅ timi lāi bhannu pāunna.

12. WHEN WE COME FROM DEHRA DUN WE WILL GET TEN DAYS' LEAVE.
Dehra Dun bāti āera das din ko chutti (bidā) pāulā.

13. ONE CAN GO OUT SHOOTING IN NEPAL.
Gurkhā māṅ shikār khelnu pāunchha.

14. PLEASE MAKE THEM COME HERE AT TEN O'CLOCK.
Uni haru lāi yahāṅ das baje āunu pathāuṇu holā.

LESSON 26

VOCABULARY

service—*nokari* in service—*bharti bhāko*

TILL, UNTIL, AS LONG AS, AFTER

In order to render the sense of TILL, UNTIL in sentences such as the English SIT HERE UNTIL I COME, the Nepalese say SIT HERE UNTIL I DON'T COME, the words UNTIL I DON'T COME being rendered by the special Past participle used to form the Past tenses of the verb in the negative, i.e. *na ā* (*ko*) *samma.* The above sentence would therefore be translated—

Maṅ na ā (*ko*) *samma yahāṅ bas*

UNTIL THE GENERAL SAHAB COMES, YOU MAY SIT—*General Sāhab na āunu bhā samma* (*na pālnu bhā samma*) *timi haru basnu pāunchha*

An alternative form which is not used much but is found more in the Eastern speech than that of Western Nepal, is—

in place of	*na āyā* (*ā ko*) *samma*	use	*na āunjiāl samma*
,, ,,	,, *na gariā* (*ko*) *samma*	,,	*na garanjiāl samma*
,, ,,	,, *na basiā* (*ko*) *samma*	,,	*na basanjiāl samma*
,, ,,	,, *na banā* (*ko*) *samma*	,,	*na banāunjiāl samma*
,, ,,	,, *na bhā* (*ko*) *samma*	,,	*na hunjiāl samma*

In order to render AS LONG AS we employ precisely the same construction as above with the exception that the Past participle is put in the Positive instead of the Negative, e.g.,

AS LONG AS I AM HERE YOU MAY SIT—*Maṅ yahāṅ bhā samma* (*hunjiāl samma*) *timi haru basnu pāunchha*

To render AFTER with a verb we either use the Past participle *garera, garikana,* or we use the word *pachi*—AFTER with the Past Indicative of the verb, e.g.,

AFTER HE DID IT—*U le gario pachi*

Sentences

English

1. You cannot go on leave until you have done three years' service.
2. We will not get an opportunity of drinking water until we reach Dehra Dun.
3. Do not come here until five o'clock.
4. As long as I am here you may not do that.
5. As long as our men are on the hills the enemy cannot advance.

Nepali

1. Tin sāl nokari na gariā samma timi chutti māṅ jānu pāunna (pāundaina).
2. Hami Dehra Dun māṅ na pugiā (ko) samma pāni khānu pāune chhaina.
3. Pānch na bajiā (ko) samma yahāṅ na āijā.

4. Maṅ yahāṅ bhā samma (hunjiāl samma) timi le testo garnu pāunna (**Eastern :** pāundaina).

5. Hamro mānchhe haru dāṅrā dāṅrā māṅ bhā samma (hunjiāl samma) bairi haru (dushman) barhnu pāunna (**Eastern :** pāundaina).

LESSON 27

THE SUBJUNCTIVE MOOD WITH CONDITIONAL

The written form of the adjectival Past participle *gariāko* which we have continually employed in previous lessons is usually *garieko* ; similarly *basiāko* becomes *basieko, bhaniāko—bhanieko* and so on. If we omit the *ko* from this last word we get *bhanie* which therefore means HAVING SAID or SAYING.

To form the Subjunctive in any tense therefore we add the word *bhanie* to the normal forms of the verb, with the exception that in the Future Subjunctive we add *bhanie* to the Past Indicative tense of the verb:

IF HE COMES TOMORROW (future)—*U* (or *tio*) *bholi āyo bhanie* which literally means: TOMORROW HAVING SAID (SAYING) HE HAS COME.

IF THOU COMEST TOMORROW—*Taṅ bholi āis bhanie*
and not *U bholi āulā bhanie* or *Taṅ bholi āulās bhanie* which means IF HE IS WILLING TO COME TOMORROW, IF THOU ART WILLING TO COME TOMORROW.

IF HE HAS GONE TO THE BAZAR RETURN HERE is therefore rendered *Tio pasal māṅ gā* (*ko*) *chha bhanie yahāṅ pharki* (*pharkera āijā*) and not *Tio pasal māṅ gayo bhanie* which would mean IF HE GOES TO THE BAZAR (in the future). It is most important to master this.

To form the Past Perfect Subjunctive IF HE HAD DONE we use quite a different construction, employing the past root of the verb TO BE—*bhā* instead of *bhanie,* together with the Past participles of the main verb, e.g.,

IF HE HAD DONE—*U le gariā* (*ko*) *bhā*
IF HE HAD NOT COME—*U na āyā* (*ā*) (*ko*) *bhā*
IF YOU HAD NOT SPOKEN—*Taṅ na boliā* (*ko*) *bhā*

The Past Conditional tense, as explained in Lesson 12, more often than not follows the Past Perfect Subjunctive clause as above. Thus,

IF HE HAD NOT COME I SHOULD HAVE RUN AWAY—
U na āyā (*ā*) (*ko*) *bhā maṅ bhāgne thieṅ*

Similarly, IF THE DOCTOR HAD NOT COME HE WOULD HAVE DIED—
Dāktar na āyā (ko) bhā u marne thio

Note the idiom IF THAT IS THE CASE—*Teso bhā* (Lesson 51, 12).

NOTE: In both forms of the Subjunctive as explained above, the word *dekhi*—(lit.) HAVING SEEN—may be added after the *bhanie* or after the *bhā*, e.g.,

Bholi āyo bhanie dekhi—IF HE COMES TOMORROW

Na ubhiā (ko) bhā dekhi—IF HE HAD NOT STOOD UP, etc., etc.

Alternative form of Past Perfect Subjunctive IF HE HAD, etc. instead of the form *na gariā (ko) bhā (dekhi)* used above, we find the form *na gariā (ko) hundo ho*. This is very common among Thaukuris and Chettris. This form is usually (not always) employed in the sense of locality, e.g.,

IF HE HAD COME HERE—*Yahāň ā ko hundo ho*

IF THERE WERE A CINEMA HERE—*Yahāň senima hundo ho*

The above Past Perfect Subjunctive construction (2 alternatives) can also be employed in the habitual sense, in which case we use the inflected Infinitive (*garne*) instead of the Past participle, e.g.,

IF HE HAD LIVED IN DEHRA DUN (habitual)—*U Dehra Dun māň basne bhā (dekhi)*

IF HE HAD HAD THREE SONS (habitual)—*Usko tinota chorā hune bhā*

(In the above sentence *hune* is often omitted.)

IF HE HAD BECOME RICH (habitually)—*U dhani hune bhā (dekhi)*

IF WE HAD SLOPED ARMS IN OUR REGIMENT (habitual)—
Hamro paltan māň "slope arms" garne bhā (dekhi)

LESSON 28

VOCABULARY

to rain—*pāni parnu* fruit—*phal phul*

THE SUBJUNCTIVE MOOD WITH CONDITIONAL—(*Contd.*)

Use of the word *po* with the Past Perfect Subjunctive IF HE HAD DONE

The word *po* emphasises the word before it, e.g.,

Yahāň po raichha—IT IS ACTUALLY HERE

If therefore we use *po* with the Past Perfect (Subjunctive), we get

Gariā (ko) bhā po—IF ONLY HE HAD DONE IT

This use is very common in speech.

IF ONLY HE HAD ARRIVED TODAY—*Āju āipugiā (ko) bhā po*

When *po* is used as above the word *dekhi* cannot be employed after *bhā*.

In the habitual sense:

IF ONLY THEY WERE TO INCREASE OUR PAY—*Hamro talab (khānki) barhāune bhā po*

In both the above cases, i.e. Non-habitual:

Āju āipugiā (ko) bhā po

and Habitual:

Hamro talab barhāune bhā po ;

in speaking, the *bhā* is often left out: *āipugiā po, gariā po, barhāune po, āune po,* etc., etc.

With the verb *pāunu*—TO BE ABLE (opportunity or permission), or TO FIND, GET:

IF ONLY WE COULD GET SOME FRUIT (habitual)—*Phal phul pāune bhā po*

but Non-habitual:

IF ONLY WE HAD BEEN ALLOWED TO SMOKE—*Cigarette khānu pāyā (ko) bhā po*

is contracted to *Cigarette khānu pā po*

i.e. *pāyā (pā) bhā po* contracted to *pā po* ; *pāyā bhā* contracts to *pā* (Negative, *na pā*).

IF ONLY WE HAD NOT BEEN ALLOWED TO SMOKE—*Cigarette khānu na pā (po)*

Sentences

English

1. If it rains tomorrow I shall not go.
2. If he is willing to come it will be all right.
3. If they have gone on leave it will be difficult to call them.
4. If they had told me I would not have gone down the hill.
5. If only they would raise our pay (Habitual).
6. It would have been all right if only they had done it like that.

NEPALI

1. Bholi pāni pario bhanie (dekhi) (ta) maṅ jānna (jāne chhaina).
2. Tio āulā bhanie thik holā.
3. Chutti māṅ gā (ko) chha bhanie (ta) bolāunu gāro holā.
4. Maṅ lāi bhaniā (ko) bhā (ta) maṅ undho jharne thina.
5. Hamro talab barhāune po (bhā po).
6. Teso gariā po hune thio.
   (Note here the use of *hunu*—TO BE, to mean TO BE ALL RIGHT, O.K.)

LESSON 29

VOCABULARY

to mind—*dhandā mānnu* late—*abelā* to meet—*bhetnu*

The use of *pani*—ALSO to mean IN SPITE OF, WHETHER......OR NOT, EVEN IF (THOUGH)

The word *pani*—ALSO used with the adjectival Past participle of a verb gives the sense of IN SPITE OF, WHETHER.........OR NOT, EVEN IF, e.g.,

IN SPITE OF TELLING THEM MANY TIMES—*Uni haru lāi dherai pāli bhaniā (ko) pani*

This construction cannot be used when there is no verb, such as in the English IN SPITE OF HIM. In this case we might change the sentence to

IN SPITE OF HIM BEING THERE, etc.—*U tahāṅ bhā pani*

WHETHER IT RAINS OR NOT (IN SPITE OF IT RAINING OR NOT) I SHALL GO—*Pāni pariā (ko) pani na pariā (ko) pani maṅ jāuṅlā*

Note the idiom:—WHATEVER HAPPENS—*Je bhā pani*

WHATEVER HE SAYS (IN SPITE OF WHATEVER) I SHALL NOT LISTEN—*U le je bhaṅiā (ko) pani maṅ sundaina*

EVEN IF THAT IS THE CASE—*Testo (teso) bhā pani. Tai pani*

Sentences

ENGLISH

1. In spite of my father coming here I shall not be able to meet him.
2. In spite of it being late we must go to Dehra Dun now.

3. Even if they don't do it it will be all right.
4. Whether the war finishes or not I shall go to Nepal.
5. Even if he does that I don't mind.
6. Whatever number of men had come (in spite of) he would have taken them all to Gorakhpore.
7. Even if there is no bazar it will be O.K.
8. It is not really necessary to do it (Even if you don't do it it will be O.K.).

NEPALI

1. Mero bābu yahāṅ āyā (ā) pani maṅ un lāi bhetnu pāune chhaina.
2. Abelā bhā pani aile Dehra Dun (māṅ) jānu parchha.
3. Na gariā pani hunchha.
4. Laṅrāi sakiā pani na sakiā pani maṅ Gurkhā (māṅ) jāuṅlā.
5. Teso gariā pani maṅ ta dhandā māndaina.
6. Jati mānchhe āyā (ā) pani sabai lāi Gorakhpore māṅ lāne thio.
7. Pasal (bazār) na bhā pani hunchha.
8. Na gariā pani hunchha.

LESSON 30

Special uses of the words *ni, ta, na, re, ke, ki, ke re* and *ra*

The correct use of the above little sounds is most important and a student who having mastered them can employ them in his speech has reached a stage where he is beginning to speak like a Gurkha. They are all very colloquial and much used.

(1) *ni*—This can be added to any tense of any verb except the Imperative and Participles, in order to emphasise. It is very commonly used. It gives the idea of the English OF COURSE or YOU KNOW, e.g.,

OF COURSE YOU CAN GET THEM IN THE BAZAR

—*Bazār māṅ pāunchha ni!*

I SHALL COME TOMORROW (OF COURSE, DON'T FORGET)

—*Maṅ bholi āuṅlā ni*

Note the slightly stronger form with *ta* (THEN, THEREFORE).

DON'T BE STUPID, OF COURSE HE IS IN THE HOUSE

—*Ghar māṅ chha ta ni*

OF COURSE HE LIVES IN DEHRA DUN

—*Dehra Dun māṅ baschha (ta) ni*

(2) *na*—This sound is used to emphasise or strengthen the Imperative, e.g.,

DO IT QUICKLY THEN—*Chito gar na*

SIT HERE, YOU MEN (plural), FOR GOODNESS SAKE
—*Yahāṅ basa na*

Another common form is made by inserting the letter *o* between the Imperative and *na*, e.g.,

SAY IT NOW—*Aile bhan-o-na*

This last form cannot be used with the plural Imperative.

(3) *re*—This little word *at the end* of a sentence shows that the speaker is passing on some words of fact that he has recently heard someone else say or has read in some book or document; i.e. it is used when passing on information recently acquired. It is allied to the *raichha* construction, studied fully in Lesson 17. Thus,

Yahāṅ na bas means DON'T SIT HERE, an order given on the speaker's own initiative, but

Yahāṅ na bas re immediately shows that the speaker is acting as a post office by passing on an order received from his superior. It therefore lends weight to the order in question.

(4) *ke*—This word literally means WHAT? but is often used in the sense of ISN'T IT?, YOU KNOW, DON'T YOU?, e.g.,

THERE IS A BAZAR IN THE VALLEY, ISN'T THERE? WELL GO THERE AND BUY ME SOME CIGARETTES—*Kholsā māṅ pasal chha ke? Tahāṅ gaiera maṅ lāi cigarette kinera leide*

(5) *ki*—This word literally means OR and is used very much in the same way as *ke* in the example given above, e.g.,

IS HE THERE OR NOT?—*Tahāṅ chha ki* (short for *Tahāṅ chha ki chhaina*; i.e. IS HE THERE OR NOT THERE?)

IS THERE A BAZAR IN THE VALLEY OR NOT?—*Kholsā māṅ pasal chha ki* (*chhaina*)?

(6) *ke re*—This is really a combination of (3) and (4) above. At the end of a sentence it gives the idea of some doubt, literally meaning WHAT IS THAT YOU SAY? as if expecting contradiction, e.g.,

HE IS IN HIS HOUSE, I THINK—*U āphnu ghar māṅ chha ke re*

I DON'T THINK WE SHOULD DO THAT—*Teso garnu hunna* (*hundaina*) *ke re*

(7) *ra*—literally means AND being used to join two words together and *not* two clauses, e.g.,

YOU AND I—*Timi ra maṅ*

When placed at the end of a statement it turns that statement into a question in which the speaker considers the true facts to be the opposite to that indicated in his statement, e.g.,

YOU CAN GET IT IN THE BAZAR—*Bazār (pasal) māṅ pāunchha*
But, DO YOU REALLY THINK YOU CAN GET IT IN THE BAZAR?
—*Bazār māṅ pāunchha ra*?

i.e., YOU CAN GET IT IN THE BAZAR and (what more)?

In the Negative:

DO YOU MEAN TO SAY THE SUBADAR ISN'T IN HIS HOUSE?—
Subadar Sāhab āphnu ghar māṅ hunu hunna ra?

LESSON 31

VOCABULARY

order—*hukam*
to order—*hukam dinu, arhāunu*
to be forbidden—*hukam na hunu*
week—*sātā*
from (of time, (E) of place)—*dekhi, dekhin*

Sentences introducing uses of *ni, ta, na, re, ke, ki, ke re* and *ra*, as studied in previous lesson.

1. HE HAS THREE SONS, YOU KNOW.
Usko tinota chorā chha ni.

2. MY FATHER IS NOT AT HOME, YOU KNOW.
Mero bābu ghar māṅ hunu hunna ni.

3. IN THIS REGIMENT YOU ARE NOT ALLOWED TO DO THAT, YOU KNOW.
Yo paltan māṅ testo garnu hukam chhaina ni.

4. YOU CAN GET CIGARETTES IN THE COFFEE SHOP OF COURSE.
Coffee shop (*kāfis*) *māṅ cigarette pāunchha ni* (*ta ni*).

5. I TELL YOU HE IS NOT THERE.
Tahāṅ chhaina ni.

6. GIVE IT TO HIM QUICKLY THEN.
U lāi chito dio na.

7. FOR GOODNESS SAKE PITCH THE TENT NOW.
Pāl aile tāngo na.

8. DON'T DO THAT!
Teso na garna (*garo na*).

9. IT IS SAID WE SHALL GET LEAVE FROM TOMORROW.
Bholi dekhi chutti (bidā) pāunchha re.

10. THEY SAY THERE IS A SMALL VILLAGE ON THE FAR SIDE OF THE RIVER.
Kholā pāri sāno gāuṅ chha re.

11. YOU KNOW THAT A HUNDRED MEN CAME HERE YESTERDAY, DON'T YOU? WELL, THEY ARE ALL RECRUITS.
Hiju sāuota mānchhe ā (ko) thio ke. Uni haru jammai rakrut hune raichha.

12. HAS THE GENERAL SAHAB ARRIVED YET?
General sāhab āipugnu bhā chha ki?

13. IS YOUR HOME IN NEPAL?
Timro ghar Gurkhā māṅ chha ki?

14. I DON'T BELIEVE THERE ARE ANY JAPS IN THE JUNGLE!
Jangal māṅ Jāpan haru chhaina ke re! (chhaina holā ke re).

15. I THINK IT IS GOING TO RAIN.
Aile pāni parchha ke re.

16. DO YOU REALLY THINK GURKHAS ARE MOHAMADANS?
Gurkhāli Musalmān hunchha ra?

17. DO YOU MEAN TO SAY HE IS NOT IN THE BARRACK?
Bārik māṅ chhaina ra?

18. ARE THERE NOT SEVEN DAYS IN A WEEK?
Sātā māṅ sāt din hunna ra?

LESSON 32

VOCABULARY

havrrsack—*jholā, jholi*
food, edibles—*khāne kurā*
goods, stores—*māl*
cart—*gārā*
to load—*lādnu*
to cause to load—*ladāunu*
to search, try—*khojnu*
to find, come across—*phelā pārnu*
land—*zamin*
to ask for, demand—*māngnu*
to cause to eat, feed—*khuāunu*
head man—*mukhiā*

Bharnu (tr.)—TO FILL, COMPLETE, LOAD.
Barhnu (intr.)—TO ADVANCE, INCREASE, GROW.

It is important that the above two verbs together with connected words should not be confused. These are as follows:—

(1) *Bharnu*—TO FILL, COMPLETE, LOAD transitively (Causative *Bharāunu*—TO CAUSE TO BE FILLED, etc.)

HE FILLED THE BUCKET—*U le bālti bhar dio*

Bharti—ENLISTMENT—literally, a filling of the unit with personnel.

Bhari (adj.)—COMPLETE, or WHOLE

Rāt bhari—THE WHOLE NIGHT

Jangal bhari—THE WHOLE JUNGLE

NOTE:—*Rāt*—NIGHT ; *rāti*—BY NIGHT ; *diuńso*—BY DAY.

(2) *Barhnu* (intr.)—TO ADVANCE, INCREASE, GROW, e.g.,

OUR REGIMENT IS ADVANCING—*Hamro paltan* (*agāri*) *barhi rahā chha*

HIS PAY HAS INCREASED—*Usko talab barhiā* (*ko*) *chha*

MY SON HAS GROWN A LOT—*Mero choro dherai barhiā* (*ko*) *chha*

The transitive form *barhāunu* means TO CAUSE TO ADVANCE, INCREASE, etc.

WE MUST INCREASE HIS PAY—*Usko talab barhāunu pario*

Barhti—ADVANCEMENT, PROMOTION, not to be confused with *bharti* explained above. This word is not used much but when used usually refers to increase of pay rather than promotion in rank.

Barhdā—TOO MUCH (Urdu *Ziāda*), MORE

HE GAVE THE SERVANT TOO MUCH—*Chākar lāi barhdā dio*

FIVE RUPEES IN EXCESS—*Pānch rupiā barhdā*

THERE ARE TOO MANY MEN HERE—*Yahāń mānchhe barhdā bho*

NOTE: TOO LITTLE—*ghati* from the verb *ghatinu* (intr.)—TO DECREASE. Trans. form *ghatāunu* :

WE MUST DECREASE HIS PAY—*Usko talab ghatāunu pario*
(Note the tendency to omit pronouns).

Sentences

English

1. You must fill your haversack with food.
2. On arriving on the hill he loaded his rifle.
3. He loaded the goods (stores) on to the cart.
4. It is three years since I enlisted.
5. In spite of searching the whole jungle he did not find it.
6. The regiment is advancing tomorrow morning.
7. Since last year his land has increased.
8. I have come to ask for an increase in pay.

9. He gave the dog too much meat.
10. The village headman caused the number of houses in the village to increase.

NEPALI

1. Timro jholā māṅ khāne kurā bharnu pario.
2. Dāṅrā māṅ āera āphnu rifle bhario.
3. Māl haru gārā māṅ bhario (ladāio).
4. Maṅ bharti bhāko tin sāl (barkha) bho.
5. Jangal (ban) bhari khojiā pani phelā pārina.
6. Bholi bihāno hamro paltan barhne chha.
7. Por dekhi usko zamin barhiā (ko) chha.
8. Maṅ barhti māngnu āko (chhu).
9. Kukur lāi māsu barhdā khuāi dio.
10. Gāuṅ ko mukhiā le gāuṅ māṅ ghar barhāi dio.

LESSON 33

VOCABULARY

elder sister—*didi*
younger sister—*baini*
book—*kitāb, postak*
punishment—*sazā*
a moment—*ek chin*
to aim—*sist linu, tāknu*
peak, top of hill—*tuppa*

Liāunu, liera āunu, leidinu—TO BRING

linu—TO TAKE, HOLD, CARRY (with *jānu*, i.e. *linu jānu*—TO FETCH)

lānu—TO TAKE WITH, IN COMPANY (Infinitive and Present tense only, for other tenses use *lejānu* or *lagnu*)

lejānu, *lagnu* —TO TAKE AWAY, REMOVE ; also TO TAKE WITH, IN COMPANY WITH in Past and Future tenses

lāunu, *lagāunu* —TO APPLY, CAUSE TO BEGIN, ATTACH OR WEAR (clothing)

lāgnu—TO BE APPLIED (intr. of *lagāunu*) PROCEED, BEGIN

The above group of verbs is very confusing to students and should be carefully studied.

Liāunu and *liera āunu* are compounds of TAKING and COMING, whilst the third form *leidinu* (used much in speech) introduces the idea of GIVING.

Lānu should always be used in the Infinitive or Present (habitual) or Polite Imperative when TO TAKE WITH is implied, e.g.,

I SHALL TAKE MY DOG TO NEPAL—*Maṅ āphnu kukur Gurkhā māṅ lānchhu* (near future)

PLEASE TAKE ME WITH YOU (polite)—*Āphu sita maṅ lāi pani lānu holā*

ARE WE TO TAKE OUR GREAT COATS?—*Brandi kot lāne ho ki hoina?*

YOU MUST DRIVE (TAKE) THE COLONEL IN YOUR JEEP TO DEHRA DUN—*Karnal sāhab lāi timro jeep māṅ Dehra Dun māṅ lānu parchha*

But, HE TOOK ME TO DEHRA DUN—*Maṅ lāi Dehra Dun māṅ lagio*

WHO HAS REMOVED MY HAT?—*Mero topi ko le lagio aṅ ?*

NOTE: The use of *lagnu* is better than *lejānu*, the latter word really being Urdu, but use *lejānu* in the Imperative, *Lejā !*—REMOVE! TAKE AWAY!

In Nepal the form *lagāunu*—TO APPLY, ATTACH, WEAR is not much used, *lāunu* taking its place. The former word is really Urdu.

Lāgnu—TO BE APPLIED, BEGIN, PROCEED is the intransitive form of *lāunu* or *lagāunu*, e.g.,

HE HAS APPLIED MEDICINE TO HIS WOUND—*Ghāu māṅ ausatai lāio*

HE HAS BEEN HIT BY A BULLET—*U lāi goli lāgio*

THEY HAVE GONE TO THE LEFT—*Uni haru debre tira lāgio*

IT HAS BEGUN TO RAIN—*Pāni parnu lāgio*

NOTE: Brahmans, Thaukuris and Chettris who speak the best form of Nepali hardly touch the *g* when pronouncing *lāgio* or *lāgiā chha*, these being pronounced *lāio* and *lā chha*.

Sentences

ENGLISH

1. He had brought his sister to my house.
2. Please bring the books here.
3. Bring me a whisky and soda!
4. Hold this rifle a moment!
5. You must take aim and fire.

6. I am going to fetch the Colonel sahab.
7. The Subadar is taking his son to Nepal.
8. Are we to take rifles with us?
9. I will take you to the station.
10. He has taken his men to the top of the hill.
11. He took away (removed) the book from my room.
12. Don't take away (remove) these stones from here.
13. Please start (cause to begin) the parade.
14. It is necessary to give (apply) punishment!
15. He went away wearing his great coat.
16. The soldiers went towards the river.
17. He had just begun to speak.

NEPALI

1. Āphnu baini mero ghar māṅ liera ā (ko) thio.
2. Kitāb haru yahāṅ liāunu holā.
3. Yotā whisky soda leide ai!
4. Ek chin yo rifle li! (linu holā).
5. Sist liera hānnu parchha.
6. Maṅ karnal sāhab linu jānchhu.
7. Subadar sāhab āphnu choro lāi Gurkhā māṅ lāne chha (lānchha).
8. Rifle lāne ho ki hoina?
9. Maṅ timi lāi tesan māṅ lānchhu.
10. Āphnu mānchhe haru lāi dāṅrā ko tuppa māṅ lagio?
11. Mero kothā bāti kitāb lagio (legio).
12. Yo dhungā haru yahāṅ bāti na lejā.
13. Kawāz lāunu holā.
14. Sazā lāunu pario!
15. Brandi kot lāiera gai go.
16. Sipāhi haru kholā tira lāgio.
17. Bharkar bolnu lā (ko) thio [lagiā (ko) thio].

LESSON 34

THE *Bhanera* CONSTRUCTION

This construction is considered the most important and useful in the whole language in its colloquial form. If mastered the student will be on the way to speaking the language well.

The word *bhanera* is the past participle of the verb *bhannu*—TO

SAY or TELL. It therefore means HAVING SAID. Its literal meaning must never be lost sight of when studying its various uses as explained below. The written form of the following constructions is precisely the same as the spoken form with the exception that the other (short) past participle is employed, i.e. *bhani* instead of *bhanera*.

As regards the colloquial form some grammarians advocate *bhanera* in certain constructions and *bhani* in others. This cannot be agreed to and such teaching produces confusion of thought. In the best form of speech *bhanera* is used in all the following constructions and not *bhani*, the latter word being reserved for the written form of the language.

I. Its first use is in sentences where the English word THAT appears, such as HE THOUGHT THAT THE DOCTOR HAD COME, HE DREAMT THAT HIS FATHER HAD ARRIVED, HE OBSERVED THAT THERE WERE NO MEN ON THE PARADE GROUND, etc., etc. Taking the first of the above sentences, this would be translated into Nepali as follows:

THE DOCTOR HAS COME, HAVING SAID TO HIMSELF HE THOUGHT

We notice two points:

(a) HAVING SAID TO HIMSELF is rendered in Nepali by the single word *bhanera*.

(b) The main verb comes at the end and must be some verb indicating the working of the senses, i.e. TO THINK, SAY, BELIEVE, SEE, HEAR, DOUBT, etc., etc.

The above sentence is therefore translated as

Dāktar āyo bhanera thānio

Similarly,

HE DREAMT THAT HIS FATHER HAD ARRIVED—*Bābu āyo bhanera sapanā dekhio*

HE OBSERVED (SAW) THAT THERE WERE NO MEN ON THE PARADE GROUND—*Pared mān mānchhe chhaina bhanera dekhio*

HE SAID HE WAS ILL—*Birāmi bhaen bhanera bhanio*

I HAD SAID I WAS COMING TO SEE THE COLONEL SAHAB—*Karnal sāhab lāi bhetnu āunchhu bhanera bhaniā (ko) thien*

NOTE: When the main verb is TO SAY or TO TELL we often omit the word THAT in the English; i.e. HE SAID HE WOULDN'T COME; HE TOLD THEM TO SIT DOWN. The construction in Nepali is of course the same and *bhanera* is used. When the main verb is TO SAY or TO TELL in very short sentences only *bhanera* is sometimes omitted; i.e. *Na gar bhanio*.

II. The second use of *bhanera* is where it is desired to translate the English word IF when used in the sense of WHETHER in sentences such as SEE IF (WHETHER) THE MEN HAVE COME. The construction is exactly the same as in I above, the sentence being paraphrased:

HAVE THE MEN COME OR NOT? HAVING SAID TO YOURSELF, SEE!—
Mānchhe haru āyo ki ? bhanera her !

HE DOUBTED WHETHER THE RECRUITS WOULD ARRIVE TODAY—
Rakrut haru āju āi pugchha ki bhanera sankā mānio

We therefore have the rule that in this construction, i.e. when *bhanera* is being used as IF, WHETHER, the sentence in Nepali must start with a question.

HE DID NOT KNOW WHETHER HIS SON HAD ARRIVED—*Choro āyo ki ? bhanera tāhā pāina*

Again note the tendency to omit pronouns, especially in this construction.

III. The third use of *bhanera* is to convey the meaning of BECAUSE, the construction being the same:

I AM WEARING MY COAT BECAUSE IT IS COLD—*Jāro lāgio (lāio) bhanera kot lā (ko) chhu*

In reply to a question, WHY ARE YOU WAITING HERE? a soldier might say, BECAUSE THE COMPANY COMMANDER IS COMING—*Company Commander āunchha bhanera.*

In this use of *bhanera* it is obvious that the noun or pronoun governed by *bhanera,* i.e. the person or animal who does the SAYING TO HIMSELF must be the subject of the sentence. In the example below the *bhanera* construction cannot be used:

THE JAPS ARE RUNNING AWAY BECAUSE THEY ARE COWARDS

The Japs form the subject of the sentence whereas the person governed by *bhanera* is the speaker of the sentence who called the Japs cowards. In other words, if *bhanera* were used the sentence would be rendered, WE ARE COWARDS, HAVING SAID TO THEMSELVES THE JAPS ARE RUNNING AWAY, which is nonsense. It is also clear that in all uses of *bhanera* the subject of the sentence must be animate as no inanimate object is capable of thinking or speaking to itself. In the sentence, THE RIVER HAS RISEN BECAUSE OF THE RAIN IN THE HILLS, if we attempt to apply the *bhanera* construction, we get: IT HAS RAINED IN THE HILLS, HAVING SAID TO ITSELF THE RIVER HAS RISEN, which is obviously ridiculous and incorrect. In this case we would paraphrase the sentence:

IT HAVING RAINED IN THE HILLS THE RIVER HAS RISEN—*Lekh tirā pāni parera kholā barhio* or [*pariā (ko) hunā le*—AS A RESULT OF IT HAVING RAINED]

IV. The last use of *bhanera* is to render IN ORDER THAT, WITH THE OBJECT OF. The construction is exactly the same but in this case we put the verb in the Aorist tense (See Lesson 9):

I HAVE COME HERE IN ORDER TO MEET YOU—*Timi lāi bhetuṅ bhanera etā āeṅ*

HE HAS COME HERE IN ORDER TO PLAY FOOTBALL—*Football khelnu pāwas bhanera yahāṅ āyo* (lit. IN ORDER TO BE ABLE TO PLAY)

HE DRANK THIS IN ORDER THAT HE MIGHT NOT BE ILL—*Birāmi na hawas bhanera yo khāi dio*

LESSON 35

VOCABULARY

reason—*kāran*	to want, wish (with verb)—*man lāgnu*
for what reason?—*ke kāran le*	to want (with noun)—*chāhinchha*
to understand—*bujhnu*	destruction—*nās*
to begin—*thālnu*	to ask—*sodhnu*
alive—*jiuṅdo*	account—*hisāp*

TYPICAL SENTENCES ON THE *Bhanera* CONSTRUCITION

1. *Bhanera* meaning THAT

1. I SAW THAT THE JAPS HAD DESCENDED INTO THE VALLEY.
   Jāpan haru kholsā māṅ jhario bhanera dekheṅ.
2. THEY THOUGHT THAT THE COMPANY COMMANDER HAD COME ON PARADE.
   Company Commander sāhab pared māṅ āunu bho bhanera thāniā (ko) thio.
3. YOU DO NOT BELIEVE THAT THE JAPS ARE ON THE HILL.
   Jāpan haru dāṅrā māṅ chha bhanera timi le patiāunna.
4. WE HEARD THAT THE JAPS ARE RETIRING EVERYWHERE.
   Jāpan haru jahāṅ sukhai hati rahāchha bhanera hami le tāhā pāio.

5. YOU WILL UNDERSTAND BY TOMORROW WHY WE DID NOT GO TO IMPHAL.
Hami Imphal māṅ kina (ke kāran le) gaina bhanera timi bholi samma bujhlā.

6. THE COMPANY COMMANDER SAID WE MUST HAVE OUR FOOD NOW.
Aile khānu parchha bhanera Company Commander sāhab le bhannu bho.

7. TELL HIM NOT TO SPEAK SO FAST.
U lāi eti chito na bol bhanera bhan.

8. I DO NOT BELIEVE THAT HE IS DEAD.
U mariā (ko) chha bhanera maṅ patiāunna.

9. KNOWING THAT IT WAS LATE HE STARTED TO RUN.
Abelā bho bhanera tāhā bhaera u dugurnu thālio.

II. *Bhanera* meaning IF, WHETHER

1. SEE IF THEY ARE IN THE HOUSE.
Uni haru ghar māṅ chha ki (chhaina) bhanera her.

2. THEY DOUBTED WHETHER THE JAPS WERE ON THE HILL.
Jāpan haru dāṅrā māṅ chha ki (chhaina) bhanera sankā mānio.

3. THEY DO NOT KNOW WHETHER THE SUBADAR IS HERE.
Subadar sāhab hunu hunchha ki (hunu hunna) bhanera uni haru le tāhā pāina.

4. I WANT TO SEE IF HE IS ALIVE.
Tio jiuṅdo chha ki (chhaina) bhanera hernu man lāgio.

5. ASK HIM IF HE IS A GURKHA.
Gurkhāli hoski (hoinas) bhanera sodh.

III. *Bhanera* meaning BECAUSE

1. THEY ARE NOT FIRING BECAUSE THEY CANNOT SEE THE JAPS.
Jāpan haru (lāi) dekhdaina bhanera hāniā (ko) chhaina.
(Note again the construction *na dekhiā ko hunā le*—AS A RESULT OF NOT SEEING, referred to in Lesson 34, III).

2. HE HAS COME TO THE OFFICE BECAUSE HE WANTS LEAVE.
Chutti (bidā) chāhinchha bhanera daftar māṅ āyo.

3. I WEAR A COAT BECAUSE IT IS COLD.
Jāro bho (lāgio) bhanrea kot lāunchhu (habitual).

4. I AM RUNNING BECAUSE IT IS LATE.
Abelā bho bhanera dugriā (ko) chhu (dugri rahā chhu).

5. I WANT TO GO TO DEHRA DUN BECAUSE MY FATHER HAS COME THERE FROM NEPAL.
Mero bābu Gurkhā bāti āunu bho bhanera maṅ ta Dehra Dun māṅ jānu man lāgio.

6. I AM SITTING HERE BECAUSE THE SAHAB IS COMING.
Sāhab āunu hunchha bhanera maṅ yahāṅ basi rahā chhu (**Eastern:** *basdai chhu*).

IV. *Bhanera* meaning IN ORDER TO, WITH THE OBJECT OF

1. THE MEN FROM DEHRA DUN HAVE COME HERE IN ORDER TO PLAY FOOTBALL.
Dehra Dun bāti āko mānchhe haru football khelos (*khelnu pāwas*) *bhanera ā chha.*

2. I AM SHOWING (HIM) THIS IN ORDER THAT HE MAY LEARN QUICKLY.
Chito sikos bhanera maiṅ le yo dekhāi rahā (*ko*) *chhu.*

3. THEY ARE DOING THAT IN ORDER TO DESTROY THE ENEMY (THAT THE ENEMY MAY BE DESTROYED).
Bairi haru nās hawas bhanera uni haru le testo gari rahā (*ko*) *chha.*

LESSON 36

Revision of *Bhanera* construction, including sentences in Lesson 35.

LESSON 37

Chāhinchha—TO WANT, etc., DESIRE
man lāgnu—TO WISH, or DESIRE
māngnu—TO DEMAND, TO ASK FOR

Some confusion of thought usually exists in regard to the employment of *chāhinchha, man lāgnu* and *māngnu.*

I. *Chāhinchha,* if used with a noun, means REQUIRE or WANT:

I WANT A CIGARETTE (lit. TO ME A CIGARETTE IS NECESSARY—
Maṅ lāi yotā cigarette chāhinchha

But, if used with a verb it means OUGHT TO, SHOULD:

YOU SHOULD (OUGHT TO) SIT DOWN—*Timi basnu chāhinchha*
YOU SHOULD NOT SIT DOWN—*Timi basnu chāhinna* (**Eastern:** *chāhindaina*)

The verb *chāhinchha* can be conjugated in the ordinary way:

PAST—*chāhio*

PAST HABITUAL—*chāhinthio* NEGATIVE—*chāhinna thio*

(**Eastern**: *chāhindaina thio*)

FUTURE—*chāhelā*, etc., etc.

but is not usually conjugated with another verb in future tenses, when *parlā* should be used ; see below.

II. *Man lāgnu* is used only with another verb and means WANT TO DO SOMETHING:

HE WANTED TO SIT—*U basnu man lāgio*

I WANT TO SEE MY SON—*Maṅ āphnu choro (lāi) dekhnu man lāgio*

(NOTE: *Parnu* when used with another verb is much stronger than *chāhinchha* when used with a verb and means MUST ; *basnu parcha*—MUST SIT, but *basnu chāhinchha*—OUGHT TO SIT. Strangely *parnu* in the negative is not so strong: *basnu pardaina*—NEED NOT SIT and not MUST NOT SIT.)

III. *Māngnu* means TO ASK FOR or DEMAND and not TO WANT:

HE IS ASKING FOR LEAVE—*U le chutti māngi rahā chha*

See Lesson 24 as to use of verb *mangāi pathāunu*—TO SEND FOR.

Sentences

ENGLISH

1. He ought to go on leave now.
2. We shall require great coats in the jungle at nights.
3. I want to see if they have come.
4. I do not wish to eat now.
5. He had wanted to keep a dog.
6. My brother is asking for (demanding) a cigarette.

NEPALI

1. Tio aile chutti māṅ jānu chāhinchha.
2. Rāti jangal māṅ brandi kot chāhelā.
3. Āyo ki bhanera hernu man lāgio.
4. Aile khānu man lāgina.
5. Kukur pālnu man lāgiā (ko) thio.
6. Mero bhāi le "cigarette" māngiā (ko) chha.

LESSON 38

Certain Alternative Verbs meaning TO KNOW

Chinnu—TO KNOW FROM RECOGNITION
Tāhā pāunu (*hunu*)—TO KNOW FROM INFORMATION
Bujhnu—TO KNOW, UNDERSTAND, COMPREHEND
Jānnu—TO KNOW FROM LEARNING
Chāl pāunu—TO KNOW FROM OBSERVATION, TO NOTICE
Chitta pāunu—TO KNOW FROM REASONING OR CALCULATION

1. I DO NOT KNOW HIS FATHER.
   Maṅ usko bābu (*lāi*) *chindaina.*
2. HE DOES NOT KNOW WHETHER THE REGIMENT HAS ARRIVED.
   Paltan āipugio ki bhanera u le tāhā pāina.
3. MY FATHER DOES NOT UNDERSTAND WHAT THE SERVANT SAID.
   Chākar le bhaniā ko kurā mero bābu le bujhina.
4. HE DOES NOT KNOW HOW TO WRITE.
   U lekhnu jāndaina.
5. I DID NOT KNOW (NOTICE) HE HAD GONE.
   Tio gā ko māiṅ le chāl pāina.
6. THE QUARTERMASTER HAVILDAR COULD NOT UNDERSTAND THE RATION ACCOUNT.
   Kotmāstar haldār le rāsan ko hisāp ko chitta pāina.

LESSON 39

orange—*santalā*
bow—*dhanu*
arrow—*kāṅr*
duck—*hāṅs*
balcony—*kāusi*
ladder—*lisnu*

to come out—*niskinu*

Certain Alternative Verbs meaning TO FALL, DESCEND

Paltinu (intr.)—TO OVERBALANCE
Paltāunu (tr.)—TO CAUSE TO OVERBALANCE
Larnu—TO FALL (ON A FLAT SURFACE)
Khasnu—TO FALL (FROM A HEIGHT)
(Causative. *Khasālnu*—TO CAUSE TO FALL)
Orhlānu—TO COME DOWN ANYTHING (LADDER, TREE)

Utranu—TO DESCEND DELIBERATELY BY JUMPING (FROM A VEHICLE)

Jharnu—general word meaning TO DESCEND EITHER FROM A HEIGHT or OTHERWISE (DOWN A HILL)

NOTE: 1. *Undho*—DOWNWARDS *Umbho*—UPWARDS

2. Do not confuse *khasnu*—TO FALL with *kasnu*—TO TIGHTEN. Idiom: PUT ON YOUR BELT!—*Peti kas!*

3. *Lotnu*—TO FALL is not good Nepali.

1. HE CUT HIS LEG BY FALLING AT FOOTBALL.
"Football" khelne belā māṅ larera khuttā māṅ ghāu pārio.

2. THE ORANGES BEGAN TO FALL FROM THE TREES.
Santalā haru rukh bāti khasnu thālio.

3. HE BROUGHT DOWN A DUCK WITH HIS BOW AND ARROW.
Dhanu kāṅr hānera hāṅs khasāldio.

4. COMING OUT INTO THE BALCONY HE BEGAN TO COME DOWN THE LADDER.
Kāusi māṅ niskera lisnu bāti orhlānu thālio.

5. AT WHAT STATION MUST WE LEAVE THE TRAIN?
Kun tesan māṅ utranu pario aṅ?

6. COMING DOWN THE HILL HE BEGAN TO HAVE HIS FOOD.
Dāṅrā bāti jharikana bhāt khānu lāgio.

7. WHY DID YOU GO UP WHEN I TOLD YOU TO GO DOWN?
Undho jhar bhanera kina umbho gais aṅ?

LESSON 40

VOCABULARY

wood—*kāth*
wooden—*kāth ko*
wood (fuel)—*dāurā*
dirt, filth—*phor*
to blow—*phuknu*
cookhouse, kitchen—*chaukā, bhānsa*
a cook—*bhānse*

Balnu (intr.)—TO BURN, REMAIN ALIGHT
Bālnu (tr.)—TO BURN, TO MAINTAIN A FIRE
Salkinu (*salkanu*) (intr.)—TO BECOME ALIGHT
Salkāunu (tr.)—TO LIGHT, SET A LIGHT etc.
Polnu (tr.)—TO BURN, SCORCH, DESTROY BY FIRE
Āgo lāgnu—TO CATCH ON FIRE
Darnu—TO SCORCH, BURN

Balnu (intr.) and *bālnu* (tr.) are normally used of fire deliberately set alight:

Yo dāurā (WOOD FOR FUEL) *baldaina* means THIS WOOD WON'T BURN

WHY HAVE YOU NOT LIGHTED A FIRE—*Taiṅ le āgo kina bālinas* (meaning MAINTAINED A FIRE)

But, WHY HAVE YOU NOT SET A LIGHT TO THE FIRE? (LIGHTED A FIRE)—*Āgo kina salkāinas*

THE WOOD WON'T CATCH (FIRE)—*Dāurā salkinna*

I WILL LIGHT A CIGARETTE—*Maṅ "cigarette" salkāunchhu*

Polnu means TO BURN not of a fire but of some object in a fire:

ALL THIS DIRT MUST BE BURNT—*Yo phor haru jammai polnu parchha*

HE BURNT HIS CLOTHING (DELIBERATELY)—*U le āphnu lugā polio*

but when the meaning TO CATCH FIRE is implied use *āgo lāgnu*:

HIS HOUSE CAUGHT ON FIRE—*Usko ghar māṅ āgo lāgio* (*lāio*)

A general word *darnu*—TO BURN, SCORCH is also used, though not very common:

Usko lugā dario—HIS CLOTHES WERE BURNT

Sentences

English

1. This wood is wet and will not remain alight.
2. During the winter you must burn (maintain) fires.
3. If you blow it will quickly catch fire.
4. The cooks have lighted the fires in the cookhouses.
5. Fires are burning in all the cookhouses.
6. He burnt his hand.

Nepali

1. Yo dāurā chiso bhaera baldaina.
2. Hiuṅdo māṅ āgo bālnu parchha.
3. Phukio bhanie chito salkinchha.
4. Chaukā (bhānsa) haru māṅ bhānse haru le āgo salkā (ko) chha.
5. Sabai chaukā haru māṅ āgo bali rahā chha [āgo baliā (ko) chha].
6. Usko hāt polio.

LESSON 41

VOCABULARY

horse—*ghorā*	goat—*bākrā*
hay—*khar*	male goat—*bokhā*
queen—*rāni*	female goat—*bākri*

THE NOUN

In Nepali there is no gender and the adjective and verb do not change when qualifying nouns denoting a feminine object. Amongst Gurkhas domiciled in India a form of speech has been evolved in which the adjective is made to end in *i* when qualifying a feminine object, such as *rāmri keti*—A BEAUTIFUL GIRL. This form, however, is not found in the majority of districts in Nepal. Although there is no gender some words denoting female species do end in *i* as in Urdu, such as:

Magarni—female of "Magar" tribe
Raini—female of "Rai" tribe
Rāni—a queen
Chori—a daughter

The procedure of denoting the female sex in animals by making the name of the animal end in *i* is not good Nepali and is really Urdu ; *ghori*—A MARE, *kutti*—A BITCH are not Nepali words. *Dhāngo chāuri* are the masculine and feminine form of some animals including a DOG and CAT ; of BIRDS use *bhāle, pothi* ; of GOATS *bokhā, bākri.* A YOUNG BIRD is *challā,* not to be confused with *chelā*—A DISCIPLE OR STUDENT.

DECLENSION OF NOUNS

Nouns ending in *o* change the *o* to *ā* in the Vocative singular and all cases of the plural:

SINGULAR			PLURAL		
N.	*Choro*	SON	N.	*chorā haru*	SONS
Ac.	*choro lāi*	SON	Ac.	*chorā haru lāi*	SONS
D.	*choro lāi*	TO SON	D.	*chorā haru lāi*	TO SONS
Ag.	*choro le*	BY SON	Ag.	*chorā haru le*	BY SONS
G.	*choro ko*	OF SON	G.	*chorā haru ko*	OF SONS
L.	*choro māṅ*	IN, INTO, AMONG, ON, TO SON	L.	*chorā haru māṅ*	IN, INTO, AMONG, ON, TO SONS
V.	*e chorā*	O SON!	V.	*e chorā ho*	O SONS!

In the Locative *māṅ* can also mean AT of places:

AT DEHRA DUN—*Dehra Dun māṅ*

In the Accusative *lāi* is added for human objects but may be used for animals to particularise. With other objects it is omitted. In the Dative it must always be put in.

In the Vocative plural it is best to omit the *haru*, as *ho* denotes the plural. *Harū* is usually left out in all cases of the plural with abstract nouns:

Tin din not *Tin din haru*

NOTE: A local **Eastern** variation exists in the fact that with the word *choro* only, the *o* is changed to *ā* in all cases, singular and plural except the Nom. Sing.:

MY SON TOLD ME—*Mero chorā le maṅ lāi bhanio* (agent case)
YOU MUST TELL HIS SON—*Timi usko chorā lāi bhannu pario* (accus. case)

Sentences

ENGLISH

1. Many Gurkhas live in these houses.
2. Give my horse some hay (to my horse).
3. The queen's house is very big.
4. Oh young men, you must kill the Japanese on the hill!
5. He is sitting on the wall.
6. Is that a male or female goat?

NEPALI

1. Yo ghar haru māṅ dherai Gurkāli (haru) baschha.
2. Mero ghorā lāi khar khuā.
3. Rāni ko ghar dherai thulo chha.
4. E tithā ho, dāṅrā māṅ bhā ko Jāpan haru lāi mārnu parchha, ai!
5. U bhittā māṅ (māṅthi) basi rahā chha.
6. Tio bokhā ho ki bākri?

LESSON 42

VOCABULARY

witch—*boksi*
to be smart—*phurli garnu*
dear, expensive—*māṅgo*
only—*mātrai*

THE COMPARISON

In Nepali the comparison is rendered by the use of the word *bhandā*, present participle of the verb *bhannu*—TO SAY OR TELL, literally meaning SAYING, WHEN TALKING OF:

HE IS TALLER THAN I—*Maṅ bhandā u algo chha*

literally, TALKING OF ME HE IS TALL.

IT WILL BE BETTER THE DAY AFTER TOMORROW THAN TOMORROW—
Bholi bhandā parsi thik holā

In the Eastern form of speech *dekhi*—HAVING SEEN is sometimes used in place of *bhandā*:

Maṅ dekhi dhani chha—HE IS RICHER THAN I (lit. SEEING ME, HE IS RICH, i.e. AS COMPARED TO ME)

There is no real superlative construction in Nepali so that if we desire to render HE IS THE RICHEST we have to use the above construction, introducing THAN OTHERS, THAN ALL, etc:

U āru bhandā dhani chha
U sabai bhandā dhani chha

Note here, *Madde māṅ* (*bāti*)—FROM AMONGST

WHO IS THE YOUNGEST OF ALL YOU MEN?—*Timi haru madde māṅ kalilo chaiṅ kun ho*? (*kalilo kun chaiṅ ho*)

Sentences

ENGLISH

1. They have brought more than yesterday (than they brought yesterday).
2. The daughter is more of a witch than the mother (Nepali riddle).
3. He is the smartest man in my company.
4. Amongst a hundred men only one will be allowed to go.
5. Flour is more expensive here than in Dehra Dun.

NEPALI

1. Hiju liāko bhandā āju barhdā liā (ko) chha.
2. Āmā bhandā chori boksi (*chha* understood).
   (Answer: *Khursāni*—THE RED CHILLI, the small pips being much hotter than the rest).
3. Mero kampani māṅ u āru bhandā phurti garchha.
4. Sai mānchhe madde māṅ yotā mātrai jānu pāune chha (pāulā).
5. Dehra Dun māṅ bhandā yahāṅ pitho māngo chha (hune rai chha).

LESSON 43

VOCABULARY

line (of men or things)—*lang*
to place in line—*lang pārnu*
line (made, such as spit-locked)—*rekhā*
stick—*lāuro*
lazy, slack—*luthro*
slack, loose (of things)—*khoklo*
to see—*dekhnu*

ADVERBS

The adverb cannot be declined and as a general rule is placed before the word it modifies:

Chitto bas—SIT DOWN QUICKLY

A word or clause may be employed in an adverbial sense governing a verb by the use of the short Past participle of *garnu*—TO DO, i.e. *gari*, lit. HAVING DONE.

bes—GOOD	*besgari*—WELL
rāmro—BEAUTIFUL	*rāmrogari*—BEAUTIFULLY
prem—LOVE (noun)	*premgari*—LOVINGLY

Dushman lāi dekhne gari bas !—SIT SEEING THE ENEMY (i.e. SO THAT YOU CAN SEE THE ENEMY)

Dushman lāi na dekhne gari bas—SIT SO THAT YOU CAN'T SEE THE ENEMY

Dushman le timi lāi na dekhne gari bas—SIT SO THAT THE ENEMY CAN'T SEE YOU

DISTRIBUTIVE NUMERALS

Dui dui gari (*garera*) *ai ja*—COME TWO AT A TIME
piche—TO EACH (*phi* is not good Nepali)
mānchhe piche—TO EACH MAN
Mānchhe piche ek ek rupiā bāṅr de—DISTRIBUTE ONE RUPEE TO EACH MAN

Relative adverbs such as:

WHEN—*jaba, jaile*	WHITHER—*jalā*
WHERE—*jahāṅ*	AS—*jasto*

are not much used in good Nepali and it is nearly always possible to avoid using them by turning the sentence round to some other construction. For instance,

jaba can usually be turned to the use of the present participle: instead of *jaba u āulā*—WHEN HE COMES, use *u āune belā māṅ* *jatā* can be turned to *jāne thāuṅ* etc., etc.

The use of *jhaiṅ* (note short *a*) is better than *jasto*

sutiā (*ko*) *jhaiṅ*—AS IF ASLEEP, or LYING DOWN
kukur jhaiṅ—LIKE A DOG
kukur le jhaiṅ—LIKE A PARTICULAR DOG
maiṅ le gariā (*ko*) *jhaiṅ*—LIKE I DO
siāl jhaiṅ na karā—DON'T SHOUT LIKE A JACKAL

But, *siāl le jhaiṅ na karā*—DON'T SHOUT LIKE THE JACKAL

The repitition of the verb in the future tense followed by *jhaiṅ* gives JUST ABOUT TO, ON THE POINT OF:

U āulā āulā jhaiṅ bho—HE IS ABOUT TO COME (lit. LIKE COMING COMING)

U garlā garlā jhaiṅ bho—HE IS ABOUT TO DO IT

To emphasise an adverb, double the main central consonant; *katā*—WHITHER, emphasised form, very common in speech, being *kat-tā*.

or repeat the word; *bistārai bistārai*—VERY SLOWLY, or add *ai*, (See Lesson 3, para. 3 as to correct pronunciation), or *nai*:

chito—QUICKLY strong form: *chitonai*

The adding of *ai* or *nai* as above is not confined to adverbs. Any word such as an adjective, noun or verb can be emphasised or strengthened in the same way. It is very common in the spoken form.

Mānchhenai ho—IT IS INDEED A MAN
Aile basnai parchha—YOU MUST NOW SIT (i.e. NOT STAND)
Timinai ho—IT IS YOU

Another way of emphasising an adverb or adjective is by the use of certain words meaning VERY, EXTREMELY, etc. These are *dherai, bahatai, sārai, bignai, chaupatai* and *aghorai*.

aile—NOW *kaile*—WHEN

kaile kaile—SOMETIMES

Kaile pani with verb in the negative means NEVER:

U kaile pani āunna—HE NEVER COMES
ajhai—STILL
U ajhai yahāṅ baschha—HE STILL LIVES HERE

Ajhai is sometimes used in the sense of MORE:

Ajhai khaniā—POUR OUT SOME MORE (lit. STILL POUR).

Ajhai with the verb in the negative means NOT YET:

Uni haru ajhai āipugiā (ko) chhaina—THEY HAVE NOT ARRIVED AS YET

Sentences

ENGLISH

1. Why are you speaking so as not to be heard?
2. Run very quickly.
3. He came into the room unnoticed by me.
4. Fall in, in lines of ten men each.
5. Give each man a stick.
6. Wherever it is we can't reach it today.
7. Don't make a noise when the Colonel is speaking.
8. He is like my son.
9. When you speak it is like his father speaking.
10. That man is extremely lazy.

NEPALI

1. Na sunne gari kina boli rahā chhas.
2. Bes gari (contracted to *besri*) dugur.
3. Maiṅ le chāl na pāune gari kothā bhitra pasio.
4. Das das mānchhe ko lang pārera "fall in" garne ho.
5. Mānchhe piche ekunta ekunta lāuro de (note *ekunta*—ONE EACH).
6. Jahāṅ bhā pani āju pugnu sakdaina (See Lesson 29 as to *pani*—IN SPITE OF, etc.).
7. Karnal sāhab bolne belā māṅ khalbal na gara ai!
8. Mero choro jhaiṅ chha.
9. Timi boldā usko bābu jhaiṅ hunchha.
10. Tio mānchhe aghorai luthro chha.

LESSON 44

ADVERBS—(*Contd.*)

jhan—THE MORE, ALL THE MORE

jhandai—NEARLY, ALMOST

balla—AT LAST

koni—WHO KNOWS?

kaso, kasto—HOW? WHAT KIND OF?

kasori—HOW? IN WHAT MANNER?

kaso gari—SOMEHOW

mātrai—ONLY

tā—INDEED

ta—THEN, THEREFORE

po emphasises the word before it (See Lesson 28).

ni or *ta ni* emphasises a verb in any tense except Imperative. To emphasise the Imperative add *na* or *ona* to the ordinary Imperative:

gar changes to *gar-na* or *gar-ona* (See Lesson 30, 2).

NOTE: Imperatives ending in a vowel cannot be emphasised as above.

bhari—ENTIRE, WHOLE

Examples: *Jhan bhanio jhan sundaina*—THE MORE HE TELLS THEM, THE MORE THEY DON'T LISTEN!

Tio ta jhandai mario—HE NEARLY DIED

Hiṅrdā hiṅrdā hami balla āipugio (āipugiā ko chha)—WALKING AND WALKING WE HAVE AT LAST ARRIVED

Eti chito kasori gario ?—HOW DID YOU DO IT SO QUICKLY?

Sāhab bholi āunu hunchha ni—THE SAHAB IS COMING TOMORROW OF COURSE (YOU KNOW)

Chito garona (garna)—FOR GOODNESS SAKE DO IT QUICKLY

Jangal bhari khojio tai pani phelā pārina—THEY SEARCHED THE ENTIRE JUNGLE, IN SPITE OF THAT THEY DID NOT FIND HIM

LESSON 45

PRONOUNS

We have seen already that the first and second Personal pronouns *maṅ* and *taṅ* change to *maiṅ* and *taiṅ* in the Agent case, (*maiṅ le, taiṅ le*). In all other persons the pronoun does not change when the preposition is added. In the gen. case *mero*—MY, *tero* (*timro*)—YOUR, *usko*—HIS, *hamro*—OUR, *uni* (*ini*) *haru ko*—THEIR. In the best spoken form the pronoun does not change with a feminine object:

usko chori—HIS DAUGHTER not *uski chori*

Tio meaning HE or SHE is less respectful than *u*, but in the neuter it must be used.

Hami for I is incorrect ; always use *maṅ*.

When using the polite or respectful form of the verb (See Lesson 23) use *tapāiṅ* or *āphu* meaning YOU. *Tapāiṅ* is more respectful than *āphu*.

The emphatic form of			*maṅ*	is	*maṅai*
,,	,,	,, ,,	*taṅ*	,,	*taṅai*
,,	,,	,, ,,	*tio*	,,	*tei*
,,	,,	,, ,,	*u*	,,	*ui*
,,	,,	,, ,,	*u le* or *us le*	,,	*usai le*
,,	,,	,, ,,	*tes le*	,,	*tesai le*
,,	,,	,, ,,	*hami*	,,	*haminai*
,,	,,	,, ,,	*timi*	,,	*timinai*
,,	,,	,, ,,	*uni, ini*	,,	*unai, inai*

The relative *jo*—WHO, WHICH, *jaslāi, jasle* or *jale, jasko* etc. is not much used. The best construction is that fully explained in Lesson 15. *Jun*—WHICHEVER, i.e. *Jun mānchhe*—WHICHEVER MAN is much used in the spoken form, as also *je*—WHATEVER.

Je bhaniā pani maṅ māndaina

WHATEVER HE SAYS I DON'T AGREE (ACCEPT)

The strong form of *jasto* (See Lesson 43) is sometimes used instead of *je*:

WHATEVER HE SAYS—*Jastai bhaniā pani ;*

But, *Je bhaniā pani* is better Nepali

The demonstrative pronoun *yo*—THIS is conjugated as follows:

N. *yo*	Ag. *e le (es le)*
Acc. *e lāi* (*es lāi* is a more academic form)	G. *es ko*
	L. *es māṅ*
D. *e lāi*	

The form in brackets is used more by "line boys", or Indian-domiciled Gurkhas.

Tio—THAT is similarly conjugated:

N. *tio*	Ag. *ti le (tes le)*
Acc. *ti lāi (tes lāi)*	G. *tes ko*
D. *ti lāi (tes lāi)*	L. *tes māṅ*

Again, the forms in brackets are used in the "line-bāt" or urduised form of speech.

PLURAL: *ini (haru), tini (haru), lāi, le, ko,* etc., etc.

The interrogative WHO?:

N.	*ko*		
Acc.	*ko lāi (kas lāi)*	Ag.	*ko le* (sometimes pronounced *ka le*) (*kas le*)
D	*ko lāi (kas lāi)*		
		G.	*kasko*
		L.	*kasmāṅ*

PLURAL: Use the same as the Singular.

WHY—*Kina*; the form *ke lāi* is sometimes used.

ārko—THE OTHER

āru—ANOTHER or MORE

koi or *kei* with a negative verb means NONE:

Kei chhaina—THERE IS NONE

NO ONE—*Kei pani* with negative verb or

Koi (kei) pani chhaina—THERE IS NO ONE or NOT EVEN ONE

āphai—SELF

maṅ āphai—I MYSELF

Āphai le gario—HE DID IT HIMSELF

Sentences

ENGLISH

1. Whichever Gurkha comes you must stop him.
2. Whatever happens we must go.
3. Give him some rice to eat.
4. He beat me.

NEPALI

1. Jun (chāine) Gurkhāli āyā pani ulāi roknu pario.
2. Je bhā pani jānai parchha.
3. U lāi bhāt khuāi de.
4. Tile (e le) maṅ lāi hāndio.

LESSON 46

The following is a table of certain adverbs and pronouns in their interrogative, relative and demonstrative forms:

INTERROGATIVE		RELATIVE		DEMONSTRATIVE		REMARKS
NEPALI	ENGLISH	NEPALI	ENGLISH	NEPALI	ENGLISH	
kun?	WHICH?	*jun*	WHICH WHICHEVER	*yo* *tio*	THIS THAT	used with a noun
Ko?	WHO?	*jo* (*inflected* *jas*) *je*	WHO WHICH WHATEVER	*yo* *tio*	THIS THAT	used without a noun
ke, kie?	WHAT?					*Kiā* is Urdu
kaile?	WHEN?	*jaile* *jaba*	WHEN	*aile* *pahilo,e* *us bela* *is belā*	NOW FIRST AT THAT TIME AT THIS TIME	
kati? katti?	HOW MANY? HOW MUCH?	*jati* (*jatti*)	AS MANY AS, AS MUCH AS	*eti* (*etti*) *uti* (UTTI)	AS MUCH (MANY) AS THIS AS MUCH (MANY) AS THAT	refers to quantity, *not* size
katro?	HOW BIG?	*jatro*	AS BIG AS	*etro* *utro*	AS BIG AS THIS AS BIG AS THAT	refers to size only
katā?	WHITHER?	*jatā*	WHITHER	*yetā* (*etā*) *uta*	HITHER THITHER	used only with verbs of movement
kahāṅ?	WHERE?	*jahāṅ*	WHERE	*yahāṅ* *wahāṅ*	HERE THERE	*tahāṅ* is an alternative
kaso?	HOW?	*jaso*	HOW	*eso* *teso*	LIKE THIS LIKE THAT	
kasori?	HOW? IN WHAT WAY?	*jasori*	HOWEVER, IN WHATEVER WAY	*eso gari, esri* *teso gari, tesri*	IN THIS WAY IN THAT WAY	
kasto?	WHAT KIND OF?	*jasto*	LIKE, AS	*esto* *testo*	THIS KIND OF (LIKE THIS) THAT KIND OF (LIKE THAT)	

LESSON 47

THE PREPOSITION

In Nepali the preposition follows the word it governs and therefore might be termed a postposition:

Example: *sita*—WITH (sometimes used in the sense of TO with human objects): WITH THE MAN—*Mānchhe sita.*

Any word or words expressing a degree of relationship between the preposition and the word it governs is, as a rule, placed between the two, i.e.,

agāri—BEFORE, IN FRONT OF

Esko chār din agāri—FOUR DAYS BEFORE THIS

The word *kāṅ* (not to be confused with *kahāṅ*)—TO THE HOUSE OF or TO THE PLACE OF has a very similar meaning to "CHEZ" in French; (it is probably the short for *ko māṅ*). It is used with animate objects. It is also not to be confused with *khān* (Urdu: "KHĀNA")—THE PLACE WHERE CERTAIN PERSONS WORK or ARE TO BE FOUND; such as *mistri khān*—BLACKSMITH'S SHOP. The main difference in the two words is that *kāṅ* is used only with verbs of motion, e.g.,

I AM GOING TO THE SUBADAR'S HOUSE—*Maṅ subadār sāhab kāṅ jānchhu* (immediate future)

I AM GOING TO HIS PLACE—*Uskāṅ jānchhu*

An alternative with a similar meaning is *thaiṅ* sometimes pronounced *thim,* being generally used when referring to inferiors:

HE IS GOING TO THE DHOBIE—*U dhobi thaiṅ ga* (*ko*) *chha*

A further very common alternative is made by the use of *bhā* (*ko*) *thāuṅ* (lit.) THE PLACE WHERE HE IS, the *ko* being left out in speech. This form is much employed in central and western Nepal and is very colloquial.

I AM GOING TO THE COLONEL—*Karnal sāhab bhā thāuṅ jānchhu*

This form is usually used of superiors. Of the three constructions *kāṅ* and *thaiṅ* are not much used by uneducated Gurkhas other than Brahmans, Thaukuris and Chettris although all Gurkhas understand them and sometimes employ them. Their employment is, however, good Nepali, and they should therefore be used by British Officers. The third form, *bhā* (*ko*) *thāuṅ* is very common and may be used of inanimate objects as well as animate, e.g.,

I AM GOING TO THE PLACE WHERE THE CINEMA IS—*Senima bha thāuṅ jānchhu*

HE IS GOING TO THE REGIMENT—*U paltan bhā thāuṅ jānchha*

upranta. or *upranta kurā māṅ*—BESIDES

kāran—REASON

kāran le—BY REASON OF, BECAUSE OF

kie kāran le ?—FOR WHAT REASON?

kie kāran le bhanie—BECAUSE (sometimes used with a verb)

Timi yahāṅ basiā (ko) kāran le—BECAUSE OF YOUR SITTING HERE

But, *Timi yahāṅ basiā (ko) hunā le* would be better Nepali

teso bhā (ko) hunā le—AS THINGS ARE LIKE THAT (THINGS BEING AS THEY ARE)

NEGATIVE: *Timi le na gariā ko kāran le (hunā le)*—AS A RESULT OF YOUR NOT DOING IT

cheu māṅ—AT THE EDGE OF

nimti or *nimtā māṅ*—WITH A VIEW TO takes *ko*—OF:

WITH A VIEW TO TEACHING HIM—*U lāi sikāunu ko nimti*

pāri—THE OTHER SIDE and *wāri*—THIS SIDE (of something linear such as road, river, etc.) are used with the noun in the nominative:

kholā pāri—THE OTHER SIDE OF THE RIVER, not *kholā ko pāri*. The same applies to *bhitra*—INSIDE: INSIDE THE HOUSE—*Ghar bhitra,* but OUTSIDE THE HOUSE—*Ghar ko bāira* or *Ghar dekhi bāira.*

sātnu—TO EXCHANGE

ko sāta māṅ—IN EXCHANGE FOR

LESSON 48

THE PREPOSITION (*Contd.*)

bāto, bāti, bāta—FROM, FROM THE DIRECTION OF

When employed next to the word *bāto* meaning ROAD use *bāro*:

FROM THE DIRECTION OF THE ROAD—*Bāto bāro*

bāro also means VIA:

I AM GOING TO LAHORE VIA SAHARANPUR—*Maṅ Sahāranpur bāro Lahore māṅ jānchhu*

thāuṅ māṅ—IN PLACE OF (governs Genitive)

I HAVE COME IN HIS PLACE—*Usko thāuṅ māṅ maṅ āeṅ*

undho—DOWNWARDS

umbho—UPWARDS

sometimes also used as ABOVE and BELOW but not good Nepali if used in this sense.

I AM GOING UP THE HILL—*Maṅ umbho jānchhu*

BELOW THE HOUSE—*Ghar dekhi* (*ko*) *undho*

samma (connected with the Urdu word "SAMET")—UP TO, ON A LEVEL WITH:

GO UP TO THE FOOT OF THAT TREE—*Tio rukh ko phed samma jā*

sātha māṅ—IN COMPANY WITH (superiors) (governs Genitive):

I SHALL GO ON LEAVE WITH THE COLONEL—*Maṅ karnal sāhab ko sātha māṅ bidā māṅ jāuṅlā*

bittikai used with the inflective Infinitive of a verb gives IMMEDIATELY:

IMMEDIATELY THE SAHAB CAME THEY RAN AWAY—*Sāhab āune bittikai uni haru bhāgio*

(NOTE: The final sound of the word *bittikai* is *kai* with a short *a* not *kāi* as it is often incorrectly pronounced by students.)

When it is desired to exrpess IMMEDITELY without a verb, such as in the sentence GO TO THE POST OFFICE IMMEDIATELY use *turanta* or *turantai, chito, chāṅrai* or *jhatla.*

puṅro—ABOUT (in regard to time)

AT ABOUT THREE O'CLOCK—*Tin baje puṅro*

khātir le—FOR THE PURPOSE OF

ko lāgi—FOR THE PURPOSE OF is not good Nepali. Use either *ko nimti* as explained above or, better still, the infinitive of the verb alone. See also Lesson 34 (IV) as to *Bhanera* construction.

HE IS GOING TO THE BAZAR FOR THE PURPOSE OF BUYING MEAT—*Tio pasal māṅ māsu kinnu gā* (*ko*) *chha*

The habit of using *ko lāgi* to mean FOR in sentences such as FOR TOMORROW'S PARADE is very bad Nepali. Use *māṅ*:

Bholi ko kawāz māṅ

In good Nepali *ko lāgi* is not used.

tala—BELOW takes *dekhi*: *ghar dekhi tala.*

māṅthi—ON, OVER, ABOVE takes *dekhi* if used in the sense of ABOVE, otherwise use with the nominative.

nira—NEAR:

THERE WAS A STOOL NEAR THE BED—*Khāt nira yotā morhā thio*

tira—TOWARDS, IN THE DIRETCION OF, often employed in the sense of TO of locality:

I AM GOING TO DEHRA DUN—*Maṅ Dehra Dun tira jānchhu*

LESSON 49

VOCABULARY

cloth, clothes—*lugā*
hour—*ghantā*
to cool down, become cold—*selāunu*
to leave—*chārnu*
cliff—*bhir*
mouse—*musā*
hole—*dhulo*
rays of sun—*ghām*
to present, put forward—*thāpnu*
blanket—*rāri*
relief—*badlā*
hope—*āsā*
flower—*phul*
main road—*mul bāto*
spring (water)—*mul pāni*

SENTENCES INTRODUCING USE OF PREPOSITIONS STUDIED IN LESSON 47 AND 48

1. GOATS GO WITH GOATS (Nepali proverb).
Bākrā sitai bākrā.

2. HE WAS MARCHING 300 YARDS BEHIND THE SAHAB.
U sāhab ko tin sai gaz pachi hiṅri rahā thio.

3. IT WILL BE ALL RIGHT IF YOU DON'T GO TO YOUR FATHER TODAY.
Āju bābu kāṅ na gayā (gā) pani hunchha.
(Note use of the verb TO BE to mean IT WILL BE ALL RIGHT. This is a common use: *Dehra Dun māṅ jānu pā hune thio*—IT WOULD BE ALL RIGHT IF WE COULD GO TO DEHRA DUN).

4. THOSE MEN ARE TAKING THEIR CLOTHES TO THE DHOBIE.
Uni mānchhe haru āphnu lugā dhobi thaiṅ lagi rahā chha (or *liera gā chha*).

5. BESIDES IF HE DOES NOT COME WE SHALL GET NO MONEY.
Upranta, tio āina bhanie hami ta paisā pāune chhaina.

6. WHY DID YOU SIT ON THE GROUND?
Taṅ ke kāran le bhuiṅ māṅ basis ?

7. THIS RICE IS COLD BECAUSE IT HAS BEEN LEFT HERE FOR TWO HOURS.
Yo chāṅwal selāchha kie kāran le bhanie, dui ghantā dekhi yahāṅ chāriā (ko) chha. (An alternative to the above sentence would be: *Yo chāṅwal kie kāran le selāchha bhanie yahāṅ dui ghantā dekhi chāriāko hunā le*).

8. HE WENT TO THE EDGE OF THE CLIFF AND FELL OVER.
Bhir ko cheu māṅ gaera paltio (overbalanced).

9. WITH A VIEW TO REACHING THEIR HOMES ON THE SAME DAY THEY TOOK THE TRAIN.
Tai din māṅ ghar māṅ pugnu ko nimti uni haru rel māṅ charhio. (The above sentence is of course far better rendered by the *Bhanera* construction. See Lesson 34, IV).

10. PLEASE TAKE ME ACROSS THE RIVER.
Maṅ lāi kholā pāri tārnu holā.

11. THE MOUSE RAN INTO THE HOLE.
Musā dhulo bhitra pasio.

12. HAVING COME OUT OF THEIR HOUSES THEY WERE WARMING THEMSELVES IN THE SUN.
Āphnu āphnu ghar dekhi bāira niskera ghām tāpi rahā thio.

13. IN EXCHANGE FOR A BLANKET I RECEIVED ONE MAUND OF FLOUR.
Rāri ko sāta māṅ ek man pitho pāeṅ.

14. THE ENEMY WERE ADVANCING FROM THE DIRECTION OF THE ROAD.
Bairi haru bāto tira bāti agāri barhi rahā thio.

15. HOW MANY TIMES HAVE I GOT TO TELL YOU TO COME DOWN?
Undho jhar bhanera kati pāli bhani rahanu parchha aṅ ?

16. AS FAR AS I COULD SEE THERE ARE NO ENEMY ON THE WHOLE PLAIN.
Maiṅ le dekhiā (ko) samma phāṅt bhari māṅ dushman chhaina.

17. IMMEDIATELY MY RELIEF ARRIVES I SHALL GO ON LEAVE.
Mero badlā āune bittikai maṅ ta bidā māṅ jai jānchhu. (*jai jānu*—TO GO OFF, GO AWAY).

18. I HOPE THAT HE WILL COME HERE ABOUT THE DAY AFTER TOMORROW.
Parsi puṅro āunchha bhanera āsā gariā (ko) chha.

19. BELOW THE HOUSE THERE IS A FLOWER GARDEN.
Ghar dekhi tala (taltira) yotā phul bāri hune raichha.

20. THERE IS A SPRING NEAR MY HOUSE.
Mero ghar nira mul pāni chha.

LESSON 50

IDIOMS

A knowledge of these Idioms goes a long way towards speaking the language well.

I. ABOUT TO, ON THE POINT OF is rendered in Nepali by the word *āṅtyo*, e.g.,

HE IS ON THE POINT OF DOING—*U garnu āṅtyo*

āṅtyo is sometimes confused by students with the Imperfect or Past Perfect tense. This is incorrect, it being used as above in the sense of the Present. It cannot be conjugated nor has it a negative form. It has, however, a past form: *āṅtiā (ko) thio* (written form *āṅtye ko thio*), e.g.,

HE WAS ON THE POINT OF DOING—*U garnu āṅtiā (ko) thio*

(See also Lesson 43 regarding the use of *jhaiṅ* to render ON THE POINT OF,

2. *uile*—FORMERLY ; *uile dekhi*—SINCE FORMERLY ; *uile uile dekhi*—SINCE A VERY LONG TIME AGO ; *uile barkha dekhi*—SINCE FORMER YEARS.

HOW LONG AGO?—*Kati din bho ?*

3. *pārnu* (intr. *parnu*) means TO MAKE in a sense other than TO FABRICATE, TO CONSTRUCT, or PREPARE, when *banāunu* should be used, e.g.,

HE HAS MADE A FOOL OF ME—*Maṅ lāi baulāhā pāriā (ko) chha e !*

MAKE IT BLACK—*Ti lāi kālo pār*

YOU MUST GET IT READY NOW—*Aile taiyār pārnu pario*

THIS FOOD HAS MADE ME ILL—*Yo khurāk le maṅ lāi birāmi pāriā (ko) chha*

But,

MAKE ME A BOX AND BRING IT HERE—*Yotā bākas banāera yahāṅ lei de*

HE IS BUILDING A HOUSE—*Ghar banāi rahā chha*

4. *sukh*—COMFORT
dukh—DISCOMFORT

Jahāṅ sukhai therefore literally means WHEREVER COMFORT or WHEREVER THERE IS COMFORT. Used in this way it has come to mean WHEREVER YOU LIKE or ALL OVER THE PLACE, EVERYWHERE, e.g.,

Yo des māṅ Gurkhāli jahāṅ sukhai basiā (ko) chha—GURKHAS ARE LIVING EVERYWHERE IN THIS COUNTRY (lit. WHEREVER THEY PLEASE)

The form *jatā sukhai* with verbs of movement is also used.

The form *Jun sukhai māṇchhe*—WHICHEVER MAN YOU LIKE is used but is not common.

5. AS MUCH AS POSSIBLE, AS FAR AS POSSIBLE—*sakiā samma*

AS FAR AS POSSIBLE YOU MUST FINISH IT TOMORROW—*Sakiā samma bholi sidāunu parchha*

An alternative construction is *sakdo bhar*, Present participle of *saknu* with *bhar* or *bhari* meaning WHOLE, ENTIRE (See Lesson 32), e.g.,

AS FAR AS POSSIBLE WE WILL STAY THE NIGHT IN BATOLI—*Sakdo bhar Batoli māṅ bās basuṅlā*

but this last construction is not used generally, being largely confined to the eastern form of speech.

LESSON 51

IDIOMS (*Contd.*)

6. NONSENSE, IMPOSSIBILITY, etc.

It was explained in Lesson 28 that *hunu*—TO BE is often used to mean TO BE ALL RIGHT. NONSENSE is therefore translated by *Na hune kurā,* (lit.) NOT ALL RIGHT SPEECH (or THING), e.g.,

WHAT NONSENSE HE IS TALKING—*Kasto na hune kurā gariā (ko) chha*

IT IS IMPOSSIBLE FOR US TO REACH DEHRA DUN TODAY (lit. TO REACH DEHRA DUN TODAY IS NONSENSE—*Āju Dehra Dun māṅ pugnu na hune kurā bho (bhaio)*

WERE IT POSSIBLE—*hunu sakiā (ko) bhā ?*

7. WHILE, WHILST ; put verb in Present participle repeating it a second time in strong form:

HE DIED WHILST WALKING ALONG THE ROAD—*Bāto māṅ hiṅrdā hiṅrdai mario* (See Lesson 15 as to negative Present participle being employed to mean BEFORE.)

8. TO LEAVE is *chārnu* not *chornu* which is often employed in "line *bāt*" or "urduised" form of speech. The Past participle *chāri* literally means HAVING LEFT but is used in the sense of WITH THE EXCEPTION OF:

WITH THE EXCEPTION OF THE SUBADAR EVERYONE WILL GO DOWN THE HILL—*Subadār sāhab chāri sabai undho jharlā*

9. To render the strong negative ABSOLUTELY WON'T or ABSOLUTELY DOESN'T use the strong Present participle followed by the Present tense (habitual) in the negative:

HE ABSOLUTELY DOESN'T SPEAK—*U boldai boldaina*

HE HEARS NOTHING—*U sundai sundaina*

10. JUST, JUST THIS MOMENT—*bharkar* or strong form *bharkarai,* (See Lesson 15), e.g.,

HE HAS JUST TOLD HIM TO COME TOMORROW—*Bholi āijā bhanera bharkar bhani chha*

(NOTE: *bhani chha* is a colloquial form of *bhaniā (ko) chha* This form applies to all verbs with stems ending in consonants (See Perfect tense, Lesson 6).

11. AT LAST—*balla*:

LYING DOWN HE AT LAST FELL ASLEEP—*Sutdā sutdā balla nidhāio* (*nidhāye*

EATING HE AT LAST SATISFIED HIS HUNGER—*Khāndā khāndā balla aghāio* (*aghāyo*

12. IF THAT IS THE CASE, IF THAT IS SO—*teso bhā* (See Lesson 27)

IF THAT WERE NOT SO—*teso na bhā*

IF THAT WERE NOT SO HE WOULD NOT HAVE COME FROM NEPAL—*Teso na bhā, u Gurkhā bāti āune thino*

FOR THAT REASON—*teso bhaera*

FOR THAT REASON I MUST GO TO DHARMSALA—*Teso bhaera main Dharmsāla māñ jānu parie*

teso bhāko hunā le also means FOR THAT REASON (See Lesson 49

teso gariāko hunā le—AS A RESULT OF DOING THAT

13. The adding of *e* or in some cases *āle* to any word meaning any locality or place often gives the meaning of THE PERSON WHO LIVES OR REMAINS AT THAT PLACE, e.g.,

pasal—A SHOP ; *pasale*—A SHOPKEEPER

koth—ARMOURY or RIFLE STORE ; *kothe*—THE STOREKEEPER

bhānsa—COOKHOUSE ; *bhānse*—A COOK

goth—A FARM ; *gothālā, gothāle*—A SHEPHERD

LESSON 52

IDIOMS (*Concld.*)

14. CALLED, A PLACE CALLED, A MAN CALLED etc., etc.

This is rendered by the inflected Infinitive of *bhannu*—TO SAY, which is used like an adjective:

A PLACE CALLED DHARMSALA—*Dharmsāla bhanne thāuñ*

A MAN CALLED DALBAHADUR—*Dalbahādur bhanne mānchhe*

15. Use of verb *hālnu*—TO PUT IN in the sense of COMPLETION (See Lesson 24):

HE HAS ALREADY DONE IT—*Gari hāliā (ko) chha*

DO IT NOW, FINISH IT OFF NOW—*Aile gari hāl*

16. MUST or ABSOLUTELY NECESSARY is expressed by the negative

Past participle and the negative habitual Present of the verb TO BE:

Na garikana hunna; (**Eastern:** *hundaina*)

IT ABSOLUTELY MUST BE DONE (lit. NOT HAVING DONE IT, IT WON'T DO)

YOU ABSOLUTELY MUST SHUT THE DOOR—*Dailo na lāikana hunna*

17. In addition to the *rahanu* construction indicating continuous action (See Lesson 24) we may also use the strong Present participle with *garnu*—TO DO:

CONTINUE (GO ON) WALKING!—*Hiṅrdai gar ai!*

YOU MUST GO ON PUTTING EARTH IN THE PIT—*Khālto māṅ māto hāldai garnu parchha ai!*

18. The placing of *ek* after a number gives ABOUT. This is used only of quantity:

ABOUT THREE—*tin ek*

The word *jati* (strong form *jatti*)—AS MANY AS is sometimes added, e.g.,

ABOUT FOUR—*chār ek jati*

ABOUT EIGHT MEN CAME TO THE DOOR—*Āth ek mānchhe jati dailo māṅ āyo*

(This must not be confused with *puṅro* which is used of time. See Lesson 48).

19. FOR CERTAIN, FOR SURE—*nisse* used with a verb:

HE WILL CERTAINLY COME TOMORROW—*U bholi nisse āunchha*

khās—REAL is sometimes used, *U bholi khās āunchha*

20. OTHERWISE—*natro* (Urdu: *nahiṅ ta*):

YOU WILL COME HERE THE DAY AFTER TOMORROW OTHERWISE I SHALL TELL THE SAHAB—*Taṅ parsi yahāṅ āulās natro maṅ sāhab lāi bhandinchhu*

21. Use of inflected Infinitive of verb.

In addition to the use of the inflected Infinitive of the verb as explained in Lesson 15 we also find it used in the following:

(i) In the interrogative where in English we might use MUST, e.g.,

HOW MANY TIMES MUST I TELL YOU?—*Kati pāli bhanne?* or *Kati pāli bhani rahane?*

MUST I ALSO GO?—*Maṅ pani jāne?*

(ii) When exhibiting slight indignation or surprise in the positive, e.g.,

AND I TELLING THEM THOUSANDS OF TIMES!—*Hazār pāli bhani rahane!*

This construction is very common in the spoken form of the language.

22. EVERY, of time or period:

EVERY MORNING—*bihāno bihāno*

EVERY EVENING—*beluki beluki*

EVERY DAY—*din din* or *dine piche*

23. SOME ONE OR OTHER—*koi na koi:*

SOME GURKHA OR OTHER IS BOUND TO COME—*Koi na koi Gurkhāli nisse āulā*

SOMETHING OR OTHER—*kei na kei*

THEY ARE BOUND TO BREAK SOMETHING—*Kei na kei kamlang kumlung pārlā* (*Kamlang kumlung pārnu,* slang for TO BREAK or SMASH UP)

24. We have already seen (Lesson 22) that one of the Present participles of *hunu*—TO BE is *hundā kheri*—WHILE BEING, AT THE TIME OF BEING; *chandā kheri* however gives the idea of WHILE STILL. It is not very common:

WHILE STILL IN THE JUNGLE—*Jangal māṅ chandā kheri*

WHILE YET ALIVE—*Jiuṅdo chandā kheri*

A more common construction however giving the same meaning is:

Jangal māṅ hundā hundai

Jiuṅdo hundā hundai, etc., etc.

(This latter is explained in Lessons 15 and 51, 7).

25. *chattai* with a negative verb gives NOT AT ALL:

HE DOES NOT SPEAK OUR LANGUAGE AT ALL—*U hamro kurā chattai boldaina*

LESSON 53

VOCABULARY

animal—*pasu*	to save (money), earn—*kamāunu*
somebody—*kasai*	to move (tr.)—*sārnu*
eldest brother—*jeto*	to move (intr.), to be moved—*sarnu*

SENTENCES TO BRING OUT THE USE OF IDIOMS STUDIED IN LESSONS 50-52.

1. THE MEN WHO HAVE COME FROM DEHRA DUN ARE ON THE POINT OF HAVING THEIR FOOD.

Dehra Dun bāti āko mānchhe haru bhāt khānu āṅtyo (*khālā khālā jhaiṅ bho*).

2. FORMERLY WE NEVER USED TO DO THIS IN OUR REGIMENT.
Hamro paltan māṅ uile esto gardaina thio.

3. EVERYTHING MUST BE MADE READY BEFORE THE GENERAL ARRIVES
Janral sāhab na āundai sabai kurā haru taiyār pārnu pario.

4. THE ANIMALS HAVE STRAYED IN ALL DIRECTIONS.
Pasu haru jatā sukhai phailiā (ko) chha.

5. AS FAR AS POSSIBLE LET NO ONE KNOW THAT THIS HAS HAPPENED.
Esto bhā chha bhanera sakiā samma kasai le tāhā na pāwas.

6. DON'T TALK NONSENSE!
Na hune kurā na gar ai!

(If referring to continuous speech double *na hune*, i.e., *Na hune, na hune kurā kina gari rahā chha?*—WHY ARE YOU GOING ON TALKING SUCH RUBBISH?)

7. WITH THE EXCEPTION OF MY ELDEST, ALL MY SONS HAVE DIED BEFORE REACHING THIRTY.

Jeto chaiṅ chāri mero sabai chorā haru tis sāl na pugdai mariā (ko) chha.

8. SINCE HIS MOTHER DIED HE ABSOLUTELY DOESN'T SPEAK.
Āmā mariā dekhi boldai boldaina.

9. IN SPITE OF MY HAVING JUST THIS MOMENT TOLD THEM NOT TO MAKE A NOISE THEY CONTINUE SHOUTING.
Bharkar uni haru lāi khalbal na gara bhanera bhaniā pani uni haru karāi rahā chha e!

10. AS I WAS WONDERING WHEN HE WOULD COME HE AT LAST ARRIVED.
Kaile āunchha bhanera maiṅ le thānne belā māṅ u balla āipugio.

11. IF THAT IS THE CASE I HOPE HE HAS SAVED SOME MONEY.
Teso bhā paisā kamāyo (holā) bhanera āsā gariā chhu.

12. IF THAT HAD NOT BEEN THE CASE I WOULD NEVER HAVE TOLD HIM.
Teso na bhā maṅ u lāi kaile pani bhanne thina.

13. FOR THAT REASON I MOVED MY HOUSE.
Teso bhaera maiṅ le ta ghar sāreṅ.

14. AS A RESULT OF THAT, HAVING DECIDED HE MUST SEE HIS FATHER HE CAME TO DEHRA DUN.
Teso bhā ko hunā le bābu na bhetikana hunna bhanera u Dehra Dun tira āyo.

LESSON 54

VOCABULARY

hut—*jhupro*
to run—*dāurnu*
to be angry—*risāunu*
anger—*ris*
to wander, move round—*dulnu*

SENTENCES TO BRING OUT USE OF IDIOMS—(*Contd.*)

1. THE SHEPHERDS WERE SITTING IN CROWDS IN THE HUT.
Gothālā haru jhupro māṅ thuprai bhaera basi rahā (ko) thio.

2. WE ARE LOOKING FOR A MAN CALLED DHANBIR, BUT HAVE AS YET NOT FOUND HIM.
Hami le Dhanbir bhanne mānchhe lāi khoji rahā chha tara aile samma phelā pāriā (ko) chhaina.

3. I WENT TO TELL THEM TO DO IT NOW BUT THEY HAD ALREADY DONE IT.
Aile garnu parchha bhanera maṅ bhannu gā (ko) thieṅ tara gari hāliā (ko) thio.

4. IF YOU DO NOT WANT TO BE LATE YOU ABSOLUTELY MUST RUN.
Abelā hunnas bhanie na dāurikana hunna ai.

5. GO ON WALKING TILL YOU REACH THE RIVER.
Kholā māṅ na pugiā samma hiṅrdai gar.

6. HAVING SEEN ABOUT TEN MEN WANDERING THROUGH THE WOOD THE YOUNG GURUNG GOT FRIGHTENED AND RAN TO HIS MOTHER.
Das ek mānchhe jati ban māṅ tesai duli rahā ko dekhera kalilo Gurung tarsio ra āphnu āmā bhā thāuṅ dāurikana āyo.

7. HE TOLD ME THAT THE GENERAL WOULD CERTAINLY GO TO BOMBAY ON SUNDAY.
Maṅ lāi ke bhanio bhanie Janral sāhab āitwār māṅ nisse Bombay pālnu hunchha bhanera bhandio.

8. YOU MUST STOP DOING THAT, OTHERWISE I SHALL BE ANGRY WITH YOU!
Teso garnu chārne ho natro maṅ taṅ lāi dekhera risāune chhu e!

9. AND HERE AM I CONTINUALLY GOING TO DHARMSALA AND EVEN THEN UNABLE TO MEET MY SON!
Maṅ pani Dharmsāla māṅ gai rahane tai pani āphnu choro lāi na bhetāune! (bhetne ; Alternative: *bhetnu na pāune*).

10. EVERY MORNING HE GOES DOWN THE HILL, RETURNING IN THE EVENING.
Bihāno bihāno u undho jharchha ra beluki pharkera āunchha.

11. SOME ONE OR OTHER WILL BE THERE.
Koi na koi tahāṅ holā.

12. HIS FATHER DIED WHILE HE WAS STILL AT HOME.
U ghar māṅ chandā kheri bābu mario.

13. I COULD UNDERSTAND NOTHING OF WHAT HE SAID.
U le bhaniāko kurā maiṅ le chattai bujhina.

LESSON 55

CONJUNCTIONS

1. *ani*—MOREOVER, AND, used for joining two clauses together and cannot be used to join two pronouns, nouns, etc.:

> I CAME FROM NEPAL LAST YEAR AND STAYING IN CALCUTTA SIX MONTHS I WENT TO LAHORE—*Maṅ por Gurkhā bāti āthieṅ ani Kalkatta māṅ chha mahina basera Lahore tira āeṅ*

2. *ra*—AND can also be used after a verb to join two clauses as in 1 above. In speaking it is attached to the end of the verb to become almost part of it (See also Lesson 30, 7):

> HE HAD GONE TO THE STATION AND A SHORT TIME AFTERWARDS HIS FATHER ARRIVED—*U tesan māṅ gā thiora ali kher pachi usko bābu āipugio*

ra is also used for joining two pronouns or nouns, etc., or in fact any two words:

> YOU AND I—*timi ra maṅ*
> STRAW AND HAY—*parāl ra khar*

In the case of inanimate objects the *ra* is often omitted:

> DAL AND RICE—*dāl bhāt*

3. *pani*—ALSO; with a verb, EVEN IF, IN SPITE OF (See Lesson 29):

> GIVE ME ONE ALSO!—*Maṅ lāi pani de ai!*
> I SAY THE SAME AS YOU—*Maṅ pani ustai bhanchhu*

4. *tara*—BUT used in exactly the same way as the English word BUT:

> HE TRIED TO TEACH ME BUT IN SPITE OF THAT I REALLY DID NOT EXACTLY UNDERSTAND—*Maṅ lāi sikāunu khojiā thio tara tai pani maiṅ le khās bujhina*

5. *baru*—BUT, IN FACT, ON THE CONTRARY, RATHER:

HE SAYS THERE ARE TWENTY MEN THERE BUT I RATHER THINK THERE ARE MORE—*Tahāṅ bis janā mānchhe chha bhanera bhaniā chha baru barhdā holā bhanchhu main le ta*

(Note *maiṅ le*, Agent case, in spite of Present tense to stress the pronoun, AS FOR ME, I SAY, etc. See rule at beginning of Lesson 5. The placing of the pronoun at the end for emphasis is very colloquial).

6. *chaiṅ, chāine*—THE ONE

yo chaiṅ, yo chāine—THIS ONE

tio chaiṅ, tio chāine—THAT ONE

kun chaiṅ, kun chāine—WHICH ONE?

jun chain, jun chāine—WHICHEVER ONE (relative)

(The above can all be used with a noun.)

Yo chāine mānchhe—THIS MAN

kun chaiṅ (chāine) kukur—WHICH DOG?

tio chaiṅ topi—THAT HAT

It is also sometimes used after a noun:

BRING THAT BOX THING HERE—*Tio bākas chāine yahāṅ leide*

A form is found at the capital, *chāine chāine jo ho*, sometimes contracted to *chāinjho*. It is used as a pause for breath when speaking at length. It literally means, THE ONE, THE ONE, THAT IS and is more often than not employed in speech after a participle:

MY FATHER HAVING COME HERE FROM NEPAL STAYED FOR THREE MONTHS IN MY HOUSE—*Mero bābu Gurkhā bāta yahāṅ āunu bhaera chāine chāine jo ho (chāinjho) mero ghar māṅ tin mahina samma basnu bho*

7. *ajha, ajhai*—STILL:

IT IS STILL RAINING—*Ajhai pāni pari rahā chha,*

sometimes used in the sense of MORE:.

YOU MUST STILL ADVANCE (ADVANCE MORE)—*Ajha barhnu pario*

GIVE ME SOME MORE WATER—*Ajhai pāni maṅ lāi leide*

ajhai with the verb in the negative gives NOT YET:

HE HAS NOT YET SPOKEN—*U ajhai boliā chhaina*

8. *Ki ta.........ki ta*—EITHER.........OR (emphatic):

EITHER LISTEN TO WHAT I AM SAYING OR GO AWAY FROM HERE—*Ki ta mero kurā sun ki ta yahāṅ bāti jaijā*

LESSON 56

VOCABULARY

application (written)—*binti patra*
to present, submit—*charhāunu*
to be ashamed—*lāj lāgnu* (*lāi*)
key—*sāṅcho*
padlock—*tālā*
to lock—*sāṅcho lāunu*

CONJUNCTIONS—(*Contd.*)

9. *na*......*na*—NEITHER......NOR:
na dāhinai na debre—NEITHER RIGHT NOR LEFT
na bābu na choro—NEITHER FATHER NOR SON

10. *kina bhanie*—BECAUSE (lit. IF YOU SAY WHY), but normally use the *bhanera* construction (See Lesson 34, III):

11. *siti miti*—AS A RULE, GENERALLY, used only in negative sense:
AS A RULE WE DO NOT DO THIS IN OUR REGIMENT (neg.)—
Hamro paltan māṅ esto siti miti gardaina

12. *kaso gari bhanie*—HOW (but explanation of HOW must follow); literally it means, IF YOU ASK HOW HAVING DONE:

I CAME FROM SAHARANPUR TO DEHRA DUN IN ONE DAY; HOW? BY WALKING ALL DAY LONG—*Maṅ Sahāranpur bāti Dehra Dun māṅ ek din māṅ āeṅ, kaso gari bhanie din bhari hiṅrera*

A FEW SENTENCES ON CONJUNCTIONS

1. HE CAME TO THE OFFICE AND HAVING SAT THERE FOR SOME TIME AND NOT HAVING HAD AN OPPORTUNITY TO PRESNT HIS APPLICATION HE WITHDREW TO HIS HOME.
U daftar māṅ ā (ko) thio ani tahāṅ ali kher basera āphnu binti patra charhāunu na pāera ghar tira hatio.

2. THE TWO OF US, MY SERVANT AND I, CAME TO CALCUTTA.
Maṅ pani mero chākar pani dui janā bhaera Kalkatta tira āyo.

3. I SHOULD THINK THE ONE WHO DID THIS MUST NOW BE ASHAMED.
Esto garne chaiṅ lāi aile lāj lāgiā holā bhanchhu.

4. I HAVE NEITHER A KEY NOR A PADLOCK.
Na sāṅcho na tālā chha maṅ sita.

(NOTE: TO LOCK—*sāṅcho lāunu*; YOU MUST LOCK THE DOOR—*Dailo ko sāṅcho lāune ho.*)

LESSON 57

INTERJECTIONS AND CERTAIN SLANG

Abui !—Surprise, OH!

Aiyu !—Pain.

e !—Vocative: *e tithā ho !*—OH, YOUNG MAN (never, *o tithā ho !* (o is Urdu).

he !—Respectful, often used in prayers.

āhā !—Admiration.

Hat teri !—Bother!

ie !—Comprehension. Used by an individual on comprehending something said to him which at first he failed to understand. The final *e* sound is slightly drawn out.

thu !—Disgust (pronounced *thoo*).

chi chi !—Disgust, FIE!, especially used at something vulgar or obscene.

e bābā (*bābai*)
amai (note both a's short) } exclamation, surprise ; literally, FATHER! MOTHER!

bes !—WELL DONE.

bes bho— IT IS GOOD.

e at the end of a sentence denotes slight disgust

MY GOODNESS, THEY ABSOLUTELY DON'T OBEY MY ORDERS—
Mero hukam māndai māndaina e !

lau, lā—This is used in a variety of ways ; firstly, it signifies approval, i.e. ALL RIGHT ; secondly, it is used as a sign of surprise:

Lau hunchha—ALL RIGHT, IT WILL BE

Lau, ke bhai rahā chha—MY GOODNESS, WHAT IS GOING ON

Lau khā !—TAKE THAT, THEN! (lit. EAT IT!)

aṅ at the end of a sentence denotes a question. The voice is slightly dropped (See end of Lesson 4).

Sobham—FAREWELL (as a rule, used only in writing). Note short *a*.

liāp, liāpai represents the sound of one thing hitting another, rather corresponding to the English word SLAP. *Liāp* (or *liāpai*) *pārnu* therefore means TO HIT IT CORRECTLY, or ON THE HEAD. For instance, if a man had a shot at a certain mark with a stone and hit it correctly an observer might exclaim, *liāpai pārio !* It is sometimes purposely used incorrectly with reference to HITTING A THING ON THE HEAD MENTALLY, as for instance, when a man gives the correct reply to a question ; in which case the questioner might say in fun: *Sābās, liāpai pāris.* This incorrect, though often used, employment of it gives great amusement to Gurkhas.

A word with a similar meaning but used in connection with cutting is, *kharliāpai* :

HE SLASHED THE JAP'S HEAD OFF—*Jāpan ko tāuko kharliāpai kātio*

khwāpai and *khwāpliākai* both refer to EATING, DRINKING or SWALLOWING, and mean GOBBLED UP, etc:

HE ATE UP THE APPLE—*U le seo khwāpai khāidio*

HE DRANK THE WATER IN ONE GULP—*Pāni khwāpai khāidio*

HE SWALLOWED THE MEDICINE UP—*Āusatai khwāpliākai nildio*

diānghai also refers to HITTING but hitting which would make a deeper sound than *liāpai*. It is used of firing a rifle or any weapon and sometimes of hitting with one's fists or striking with an axe. The form *dwāng* or *dwāngai* is not good Nepali.

HE BROUGHT THE RIFLE TO HIS SHOULDER AND FIRED—*Rifle kum māñ liāera diānghai pārdio*

phuta, phutai—ALL OF A SUDDEN:

HE RAN AWAY ALL OF A SUDDEN INTO THE FOREST—*U phutai ban tira bhāgio*

lutruk, lutrukai—COLLAPSED:

HE LAY DOWN IN A COLLAPSED CONDITION—*Lutrukai (bhaera) sutio*

basukha, basukhai—TOTALLY WRECKED OR RUINED takes the verb *pārnu*:

BY FIRING THEIR MACHINE GUNS THEY WRECKED THE COMPANY OF JAPS—*Āphnu M. G. hānera Jāpan ko kampani lāi basukhai pārio*

siāñtai, (siātai, Siāta)—IMMEDIATELY, QUICKLY ; an alternative form exists vide *swātai* which should be avoided, as also an anglicised form *swotai*. *Tabaka, tabakai* is also used and gives practically the same meaning. It is often used of downward movement:

Tabakai basio—HE IMMEDIATELY ASSUMED A SITTING POSITION

tiāñkai, tiākai, tiāka—EXACTLY, PRECISELY

EXACTLY THREE O'CLOCK—*Tiāka tin baje* ; an alternative form exists vide *twākai*. This form is to be avoided, as also an anglicised form, *twok, twokai*.

jhatta, jhattai—QUICKLY:

GO AND FETCH MY BOOK QUICKLY—*Jhatta gaera mero kitāb (postok) liera āes*

LESSON 58

INTERJECTIONS AND CERTAIN SLANG—(*Contd.*)

ahaṅ : (note two short *a's* and nasal *ṅ*)—NO, when used alone in answer to a question.

In reply to the question: HAVE YOU SEEN MY FATHER?—*Mero bābu dekhis ki dekhinas ?* the reply might be *ahaṅ !* (NO).

The following six expressions all have the vowel sounds *a....a* followed by *u....u*:

kamlang kumlung—SMASHED UP, BROKEN TO BITS

kharang khurung—LOCK, STOCK AND BARREL, EVERYTHING

larang lurung—LAME

dadang ra dudung—A NOISE, HUBBUB

kachang kuchung—CRUMPLED, CREASED

ghamlang ghumlung—EXPRESSES A SWAYING MOTION, SWINGING FROM SIDE TO SIDE

The following are also very useful:

dangai pārnu—TO ASTONISH

guju muju—HUDDLED TOGETHER, OR MIXED UP

ghuām, ghuāmai—MASSIVE, ROUND

āṅkhā tul tul—STARING EYES

phan phan—IN CIRCLES, WOUND ROUND

pāni pri pri parne—A VERY LIGHT SHOWER OF RAIN

pāni da ra ra parne—HEAVY RAIN

keṅ keṅ garnu—TO CHATTER, SHOUT, sometimes used of ANSWERING BACK (An alternative is *kiāuṅ kiāuṅ*)

gangan—CHATTER ; adj. *gangani*—CHATTERING

mukh kālo pārne—TO PUT TO SHAME ; (lit. TO BLACKEN THE FACE)

hairān pārnu—TO DRIVE TO DISTRACTION, TO BEWILDER

jhilli milli (*jhele mele*)—DECORATED, SMART, etc.

silika—STREAMLINED, SMART (takes *pārnu*)

thānt pārnu—TO SWAGGER, often used of dress.

swāng pārnu—TO ACT, or MAKE BELIEF, also sometims used of dress

LESSON 59

VOCABULARY

nothing at all—*kei pani* (with neg. verb).
riddle—*ān*
cut—*chot*
to separate—*chuṭāunu*
separate—*alag*
to be thirsty—*tirkhā lāgnu*
to be hungry—*bhok lāgnu*
crops—*bāli*
grandfather—*bāze*
elephant—*hāthi*
to be sharp—*dhār lāgnu*
to sharpen—*dhār pārnu*
hen—*kukrā*
to move in a circle—*ghumnu*
old woman—*burhiā, burhi*
top of skull—*thāplo*
pipe—*hukka*
guest—*pāunā*
to call—*bolāunu*
egg—*phul*

SENTENCES INTRODUCING INTERJECTION AND SLANG

NOTE: It should be borne in mind that the expressions used in the following sentences are slang and that therefore in most cases a more academic translation is possible.

1. OH YOUNG MEN, THE JAPS HAVE RUN AWAY INTO THE JUNGLE.
e tithā ho Jāpan haru jangal tira phuta bhāgio.

2. GOOD GRACIOUS, WHAT ARE THOSE MEN DOING ON TOP OF THE HILL?

e bābai tio (uni) mānchhe haru le ḍāṅrā māṅ gaera kie gari rahā chaa aṅ?

3. YOU HAVE DONE YOUR WORK WELL.
Timi haru le gariāko bes bho.

4. I HAVE HAD ABSOLUTELY NOTHING TO EAT THE WHOLE DAY.
Maṅ ta din bhari kei pani khānu pāina e!

5. SAYING IT WOULD BE ALL RIGHT HE WENT AWAY.
Lau bhanera gai go.

6. RIFLEMAN MAHABIR IS VERY GOOD AT RIDDLES.
Rifleman Mahābir le ān ta liāpai pārchha.

7. HAVING A GOOD EDGE ON HIS KHUKRI HE CUT THE BRANCH OF THE TREE OFF IN ONE CUT.

Khukri ko dhār lāgera rukh ko hāngā ek chot kharliāpai hānera chutāidio (alag pārio). (Alternative: *ek pāli diāngha pārera*)

8. BEING VERY THIRSTY HE DRANK UP THE GLASS OF BEER IN ONE GULP.

Dherai (bignai, etc.) *tirkhā lāgera bir ko ek gilās khwāpliāpai khāidio.*

9. HAVING WALKED ALL THE DAY IN THE FOREST HE ARRIVED HOME AND FELL INTO A DEAD SLEEP.

Din bhari ban māṅ hiṅrera ghar māṅ āera lutrukai nidhāyo

10. THE JAPS HAVE DESTROYED OUR CROPS.

Jāpan haru le hamro bāli busukhai pāriā chha.

11. GO VERY QUICKLY TO THE TOP OF THE HILL AND BRING THE THREE GURKHAS HERE.

Dāṅrā siāta charhera tinota Gurkhāli yahāṅ liera āes.

12. YOU MUST GO TO THE EXACT PLACE I TOLD YOU.

Maiṅ le bhaniā ko thāuṅ māṅ tiākai pugnu parchha.

13. MY BED IS SMASHED TO BITS!

Mero khāt kamlang kumlung bho e!

14. THE ENTIRE COMPANY, LOCK, STOCK AND BARREL, WILL GO INTO CAMP FROM TOMORROW MORNING.

Bholi bihāna dekhi kampani bhari, kharang khurung pāl tāngera baslā.

15. MY GRANDFATHER WALKED, LIMPING, DOWN THE ROAD.

Mero bāze larang lurung bhaera bāto bātai hiṅrnu bho.

16. GOOD GRACIOUS, DON'T MAKE SUCH A ROW!

e bābai dadang ra dudung na gara ai!

17. AS A RESULT OF CLIMBING THE TREE HIS CLOTHES GOT CRUMPLED.

Rukh māṅ charhiā ko hunā le usko lugā kachang kuchung bho.

18. THE ELEPHANT CAME TOWARDS US SWAYING FROM SIDE TO SIDE!

Hāthi chāine ghamlang ghumlung bhaera hami tira po āyo e!

19. THEY HAVE ASTONISHED ME.

Uni haru le maṅ lāi dangai pārio.

20. OUR BROTHER SHEPHERDS REMAINED THE WHOLE NIGHT HUDDLED TOGETHER IN THE SMALL HUT.

Gothāle dāju haru rāt bhari siāno siāno jhupro māṅ guju muju bhaera basio.

21. WHY ARE YOU STARING LIKE THAT?
Āṅkhā ghuāma pārera kina heriā chhas aṅ ?

22. WHY ARE YOU RUNNING AROUND IN ALL DIRECTIONS LIKE A HEN LAYING AN EGG?
Kukrā phul pāriā jhaiṅ kina phan phan ghumiā chhas aṅ ?

23. AN OLD CHATTERING WOMAN WITH FIRE ON HER HEAD (Nepali riddle).
Gangani burhiā ko thāplo māṅthi āgo. (Answer: a *hukka* or SMOKING PIPE).

24. BY DOING THAT HE HAS DISGRACED ME.
Testo garera mero mukh kālo pārio.

25. THEY BEING EXTREMELY SLACK HAVE DRIVEN ME TO DISTRACTION.
Uni haru chaupatai luthro bhaera maṅ lāi hairānai pāriā chha.

26. HAVING DECORATED HIS HOUSE HE INVITED MANY GUESTS.
Āphnu ghar jhilli milli pārera dherai pāunā haru bolāyo.

27. HE WENT SWAGGERING TOWARDS THE BAZAR.
Thānt pārera pasal tira go.

28. DON'T PRETEND!
Swāng na pār ai !

LESSON 60

ADJECTIVES

The study of adjectives has been purposely left till the last Lesson as it presents little difficulty.

In Lesson 41 it was pointed out that in the form of speech found in Nepal there is really no gender although in parts of India a form of "Urdu-ised" Nepali is found amongst Indian-domiciled Gurkhas, in which an attempt is made to employ a feminine form of the noun and adjective. This form is especially found in the written language.

The vast majority of adjectives end in a vowel sound, usually *o*. Those ending in consonants are usually Hindustani words recently introduced into Nepali.

Adjectives ending in *o* and sometimes *u* have a plural form ending in *ā*; that is, the *ā* takes the place of the *o* or *u* in all plural cases. This plural form is, however, academic and only used by Brahmans and Chettris in speech. It is recommended that the singular form of the adjective be used in the plural as far as the spoken form of the language is concerned.

Normally the adjective precedes the noun as in English, e.g.,

thulo mānchhe—THE BIG (IMPORTANT) MAN

thulo (written form *thulā* in plural) *mānchhe haru*—THE BIG (IMPORTANT) MEN

COLLECTIVE ADJECTIVES

In order to produce the idea of quantity such as in the English word MANY, i.e.,

MANY BIG (IMPORTANT) MEN WERE LIVING IN THAT PLACE the adjective is sometimes repeated:

Thulo thulo (*thulā*) *mānchhe haru teo thāuṅ māṅ basi rahā* (*ko*) *thio*

This repetition of the adjective must not, however, be confused with a similar repetition to express degree (very) with a single noun; See Lesson 43.

VERY BIG—*thulo thulo*

The following words may take the word *janā* (PEOPLE) between them and the noun which follows, provided the noun is of person, e.g.,

ALL, EVERY—*sab* or *sabai*

SOME, HOW MANY—*katti, kati*

FEW—*thorai*

MANY—*dherai*

ALL THE MEN—*sabai janā mānchhe haru*

HOW MANY WOMEN HAD COME?—*Katti janā swāsni ā thio ?*

An alternative is the use of the affix *watā* in place of *janā*. This can also be used when the noun is an inanimate object:

A FEW BOOKS—*thoraiwatā kitāb* (*postak*)

Remember, any adjective can be emphasised by the use of the termination *ai* or *nai* as explained earlier in this manual.

rāmro—BEAUTIFUL	emphasised form *rāmrai*
thulo—BIG	,, ,, *thulai*

An adjective is sometimes formed by adding *ko* to a noun:

A BRASS (adjective) DOOR—*pital ko dailo* (lit. A DOOR OF BRASS)

A WOODEN BOX—*kāth ko bākas*

(For use of Present and Past participles of the verb as an adjective See Lesson 15).

VOCABULARY

Nepali to English

L. = Lesson, tr. = transitive, intr. = intransitive,
adv. = adverb.

A

abelā—late
abui—exclamation of surprise (L. 57)
ādhā—half
agāri—in front of, forward
aghāunu—to eat to satisfaction
aghorai—very, extremely (L. 43)
āghuṅ—next year
aghi—in front of, before
āgo—fire
āhā—exclamation of pleasure, admiration (L. 57)
ahaṅ—no (L. 58)
ai—emphasises imperative (L. 13)
aile—now
āimāi—a woman
āipugnu—to arrive
āitwār—Sunday
aiyu !—exclamation of pain (L. 57)
ajha, ajhai—still, more, not yet (Ls. 43, 55)
āju—today
alag—separate
ālko—tall
ali—few, a little
ali kati—few, a little
ālu—potato
āmā—mother
amai—exclamation of surprise (L. 57)
aṅ—yes
aṅ—indicates question (L. 4)
ān—riddle
andhā dhundā—blindly
anek—various
angrezi—English, English language
ani—and, moreover (L. 55)
ani kheri—and then
āṅkhā—eye
ānt balio garnu—to be determined
āṅtyo—to be on the point of, about to (L. 50)
āphai—self (L. 45)
āphnu—own
āphu—you (polite form) (Ls. 13, 45)
apugdo—deficiency, deficient
ārko—other, another
arhāunu—to order
āru—more, others (L. 42)
āsā—hope
āsā garnu—to hope
astāunu—to set (of the sun)
asti—the day before yesterday, the other day
āunu—to come
āusatai—medicine

B

bābā—exclamation of surprise (L. 57)

bābu—father

bachnu—to be saved, to remain over

bachāunu—to save, rescue

badlā—relief, replacement

bahatai—very (L. 43)

bāheṅ—left

bāhāṅ—limb

baini—younger sister

bāira (*ko*)—outside, out

bairi—enemy

bajnu—to strike (of time), to sound (of music, etc.)

bākrā—goat

baksinu—to be charitable, to be kind to (L. 13)

bālakha—child

bāli—crops

balio—strong

balla—at last (Ls. 44, 51)

balnu—to burn (intr.) (L. 40)

bālnu—to burn (tr.) (L. 40)

bālti—bucket

ban—forest

banāunu—to make, fabricate, repair (L. 50)

bāni—habit, custom

bāṅrnu—to divide, distribute

barhdā—too much, excess

barhnu—to advance, increase, grow (intr.) (L. 32)

barhāunu—to increase (tr.) (L. 32)

bāri—field

bāri māṅ (*ko*)—about, regarding, concerning

barkha—year

barkhā—rainy season, monsoon

barsa—year

bāro—via

baru—in fact, on the contrary (L. 55)

bās—halting place

bās basnu—to stay the night, halt

basālnu—to cause to sit

basnu—to sit, live

batās—wind

batāunu—to show (by explanation)

bātho—clever

bāti—from

bāto—road

baulāhā—fool

bāze—grandfather

bāzi—competition

belā—time (L. 15)

Belāet—England

beluki—evening, in the evening

bethā—illness

bes—good (L. 57)

besri, besgari—well (adv.)

bhā—if, having become

bhāgnu—to run away

bhāi—younger brother

bhāle—male bird

bhānchnu—to break (tr.) of something linear

bhandā—than (L. 42)

bhanera—that, whether, because, in order to (L. 34)

bhanie—if (L. 27)

bhannu—to say, tell

bhānsa—cookhouse, kitchen

bhānse—cook

bhari—whole, complete, entire

bhariāng—ladder (English type)
bharāunu—to cause to fill (L. 32)
bharnu—to fill (tr.) (L. 32)
bharkar—just (adv.) (L. 51)
bharti—enlistment (L. 32)
bhāt—cooked rice, food
bhatkāunu—to cause to collapse, to knock down
bhatkinu—to collapse, fall down (intr.)
bher—late
bhetāunu—to cause to meet
bhetnu—to meet
bhir—cliff
bhitra—inside
bhittā—wall (masonry)
bholi—tomorrow
bholi parsi—shortly, in a few days' time
bhuiṅ—ground
bibār—Thursday
bidā—leave
bignai—extremely, enormously (L. 43)
bihā—marriage
bihā garnu—to marry
bihā hunu—to be married
bihān, bihāno—morning, in the morning
binti patra—written application
birālu—cat
birāmi—ill
birāunu—to make a mistake
birsinu—to forget
biruwā—seedling, sapling
bistāro—slowly
bittikai—as soon as, immediately (L. 48)
biuṅjhinu—to wake up (intr.)
bokhā—male goat
boksi—witch
bolāunu—to call
bolnu—to speak
borā, bori—sack
budhbār—Wednesday
bujhnu—to understand
burho—old man
burhi, burhiā—old woman
busukhai pārnu—to wreck (L. 57)

C

chāeṅ—shade
chāhinchha—to want, ought (L. 37)
chaiṅ, chāine—the one (L. 55)
chākar—servant
chākari—service
chāl—behaviour, practice
chāl pāunu—to notice (L. 38)
challā—young bird, chick
chām chum—quiet
chaṅkhie—intelligent
chāṅro—quickly, soon
chāṅwal—rice (uncooked)
charā—bird
charhāunu—to present (cause to mount)
chāri—except (L. 51)
charhnu—to climb, ascend
charnu—to sow (seed)
chārnu—to leave
chattai—not at all (verb in neg. L. 52)
chaukā—cookhouse, kitchen
chaupatai—extremely, very (L. 43)
chāur—plain, open country
chāuri—female of certain animals

chelā—pupil, disciple
cheu māṅ—at the edge
chiā—tea
chi chi chi—exclamation of disgust (L. 57)
chin—moment
chinnu—to recognise (L. 38)
chip chipe—shallow (of water)
chirnu—to split
chiso—cold (of water), wet
chito—quickly
chitta pāunu—to know (from reasoning) (L. 38)
chopnu—to attack
chori—daughter
chornu—to steal
choro—son
chot—cut
chutāunu—to separate
chutti—leave (holiday)

D

dadang ra dudung—noise (L. 58)
dādura—measles
daftar—office
dāhi—jealous
dāhine—right
dailo—door (small)
dāju—elder brother
dān—gift
dangai pārnu (tr.)—to astonish
dangai hunu (intr.)— to be astonished
dāṅrā—a hill
da ra ra—sound of rain pouring heavily (L. 58)
darnu—to burn, scorch (L. 40)
dāurā—wood (fuel)
dāurnu—to run
debre—left
dekhāunu—to show (by pointing out)
dekhi, dekhin—from, than, since (L. 42)
dekhnu—to see
deota thān—temple
des—country
dhamki—reproof
dhan—riches, wealth
dhān—rice (growing)
dhāngo—male of certain animals
dhandā mānnu—to mind (to take exception to)
dhani—rich
dhanu—bow (arrow)
dhār—edge (of instrument or hill, etc.)
dhār lāgnu—to be sharp (intr.)
dhār pārnu—to sharpen
dhāuwa—war
dherai—many, very
dhiān dinu—to pay attention, concentrate
dhokā—door (large), gate
dhulo—dust
dhungā—stone
dhunu—to wash
diānghai pārnu—to make a bang (L. 57)
didi—elder sister
din—day
dinu—to give, to allow (L. 24)
diuṅso—in the daytime
dukhnu—to ache
dugurnu—to run
dukh, dukha—discomfort, trouble
dulo—hole
dulnu—to wander, go for a stroll
dungā—boat
dushman—enemy

E

e !—vocative case, Oh! , exclamation of mild disgust or surprise (L. 57)
esari—in this manner
eso, esto—like this
etā, yetā—hither, to here
etro—as big as this
etti, eti—as many as this

G

gāi—cow
gairo—deep
gangan—chatter (L. 58)
gangani—chattering (L. 58)
gāṅtho—knot, joint
gārā—cart
garāunu—to cause to do
gari—forms adverbs (L. 43)
garam—hot, warm
garnu—to do
gāuṅ—village
ghail bhā ko—wounded
ghāite—casualty
ghām—rays of the sun
ghamlang ghumlung—swaying, lurching (L. 58)
ghantā—hour
ghar—house, home
ghatāunu—to decrease (tr.)
ghati—deficient, too little
ghatinu—to decrease (intr.)
ghāu—wound, sore
ghorā—horse
ghumnu—to circle, wander
gohār dinu—to help
goli—ball, bullet
goth—farm
gothālā—shepherd, cowherd
guju muju—huddled together
guntā—bundle
Gurkhā—Nepal
Gurkhāli—of Nepal, Nepali language, a Gurkha (person)

H

hairān pārnu—to bewilder, drive to distraction (L. 58)
halāunu—to move, shake (tr.)
halinu—to move, shake (intr.)
hālnu—to put in, finish off (L. 52)
hami (haru)—we
hamro—our
hāṅgā—branch
hānnu—to hit, strike
hāṅs—duck
hār—bone
harāunu—to lose, misplace
harkat—movement
hārnu—to lose (battle or competition)
haru—sign of plural (L. 4)
hat teri—exclamation of annoyance, Oh bother!
hatār—hurry, haste
hāth—hand, arm
hāthi—elephant
hatnu—retire, retreat
hawas—may it be so, please (L. 13)
hazur—you (polite), your honour (L. 13)
he—respectful vocative (L. 57)
herchār garnu—to look after
hernu—to look, watch
hijo, hiju—yesterday

hijo āju—nowadays
hijo asti—some time ago
hilo—mud
himāl—high hills
hin garnu—to hate
hiṅrnu—to walk, move
hirkāunu—to hit, beat
hisāp—account
hiuṅ—snow
hiuṅdo—cold weather, winter
ho—yes, it is so
holā—probably (L. 11), please (L. 13)
hukam—order
hukam dinu—to order
hukka—pipe (smoking)
hunā le—reason (L. 47)
hundo ho—if (past conditional) (L. 27)
hunu—to be, exist, become (L. 16)

I

ini haru, uni haru—they
ita, itta—hither, to here

J

jaba—when (relative) (L. 43)
jahāṅ—where (relative) (L. 43)
jahāṅ sukhai—everywhere (L. 50)
jaijānu—to go away
jaile—when (relative) (L. 43)
janā—person
jangal—jungle
jānnu—to know (from learning) (L. 24)
jāṅr—rice beer
jānu—to go
jaro—fever
jasori—cold
jasori—whose (relative)
jasori—in *jasto*—like, as (relative) (L. 43)
jasori—in like manner, as (relative)
jatā—whither (relative) (L. 43)
jati, jatti—as many as (relative), about (L. 52)
jatro—as big as (relative)
je—whatever (relative) (L. 45)
jeto—eldest brother
jitnu—to win, conquer, beat
jiuṅdo—alive
jhaiṅ—like (relative) (L. 43)
jhan—the more, all the more (L. 44)
jhandai—nearly, almost
jharnu—to descend
jhatta—quickly
jhel khāna—jail
jhiāl—window
jhilli milli—decorated (L. 58)
jholā, jholi—haversack
jhor—bush
jhulkinu—to rise (of sun)
jhupro—hut
jo—who, which (L. 45)
jornu—to add
juā khelnu—to gamble
juāp—answer, reply
jugā—leech
jun—whichever (relative) (L. 45
juttā—shoe

K

kachang kuchung—crumpled (L. 58)
kahāṅ—where?
kaile—when?

kaile pani—never (with neg. verb) (L. 43)
kalilo—young
kālo—black
kām—work
kamāunu—to earn, save money
kamilā, kimlā—ant
kamlang kumlung—smashed, broken (L. 58)
kāṅ—at the house of (L. 47)
kān—ear
kaṅgāli—poor
kāusi—balcony
kāṅr—arrow
kāphar—coward
karahār garnu—to promise
karāunu—to shout
kāran—reason
kasai (le)—(by) somebody
kasko—whose? (inter.)
kasnu—to tighten (L. 39)
kaso, kasto—how? what kind of? (L. 46)
kasogari, kasori—how? in what manner? (L. 56)
kaso gari bhanie—how? (L. 56)
katā—to where, whither (L. 5)
katāunu—to cause to cut
kāth—wood
kathā—tale, story
katro—how big?
kati, katti—how many?
kātnu—to cut
kawāz—parade
ke ? kie ?—what? (L. 30)
ke lāi—why (L. 45)
ke re—I think, what's that you say? (L. 30)
kei—some, none (with neg. verb) (L. 45)
kei na kei—something or other (L. 52)
kei pani—nothing (with neg. verb)
keṅ keṅ garnu—to chatter, answer back (L. 58)
ketā—boy, young man
ketā keti—children
khalbal—noise
khālto—pit, trench
khaniāunu—to pour
khānki—pay
khane kurā—edibles, food
khannu—to dig
khānu—to eat, drink, smoke
khapnu—to endure (of clothes, etc.) to wear well
khar—hay
kharang khurung—everything (L. 58)
kharliāpai—sound of cutting (L. 57)
khās—real, certainly (L. 52)
khasālnu—to cause to fall (L. 39)
khasnu—to fall (L. 39)
khāt—bed
khatāunu—to detail
khātir le—for the purpose of
khelnu—to play
kher—period of time
kheri—while (L. 15)
khetālā—farmer
khoi—where is it?
khojnu—to search for, try
kholā—river
kholsā—valley
khor—enclosure, pen
khuāpai khānu—to gobble (L. 57)

khuāunu—to cause to eat, to feed
khur—hoof
khurāk—food
khursāni—chilli
ki—or, shows question (L. 4)
ki...ki—either...or
kina—why? (L. 45)
kina bhanie—because (L. 56)
kinnu—to buy
kirā—insect
kitāb—book
ko—who? (L. 46)
ko—of (gen. case) (L. 41)
koi—some, none (with neg. verb) (L. 45)
koi na koi—some one or other (L. 52)
koni—who knows?
kothā—room, house
kuhunu—to rot
kukrā—chicken
kukur—dog
kum—shoulder
kun—which?
kurā—speech, talk, language, thing

L

lā—exclamation (L. 57)
ladāunu—to cause to load
lādnu—to load
lagāunu—to apply, wear, cause to begin (L. 33)
ko lāgi—in order to (L. 48)
lagnu—to take away, remove (L. 33)
lāgnu—to be applied, to begin (L. 33)
lāi—to (dative), for, in order to
lāj—shame
lāj lāgnu—to be ashamed
lāmo—long
lang—line
lānu—to take with (L. 33)
larāi—war
larang lurung—lame, limping (L. 58)
larnu—to fall
larnu—to fight
lau !—exclamation (L. 57)
lāunu—to apply, wear, cause to begin (L. 33)
le—by (Agent case) (L. 41)
leidinu—to bring (L. 33)
lejānu—to take away, remove (L. 33)
lekh—high hills
lekhnu—to write
liāpat pārnu—to hit the nail on the head (L. 57)
liāunu, liera āunu—to bring
linu—to take, hold (L. 33)
linu jānu—to fetch (L. 33)
lisnu—ladder (log of wood with footrests)
logne, lognie—man, husband
lugā—clothes, cloth
luthro—lazy, slack
lutruk, lutrukai—exhausted (L. 57)

M

madde māñ—among
makinu—to rot (clothes or equipment)
māl—goods, stores
malnu—to rub, polish

mań—I
man—mind
man lāgnu—to want, wish (L. 37)
māń—in, to (of places) at, on
mānchhe—person, man
māngnu—to demand, ask for (L. 37)
māńgo—dear (of price)
manjuri—approval
mānnu—to obey, consider
māńthi—above, on
marnu—to die
mārnu—to kill
māsu—meat, flesh
mātrai—only
māuri—bee
mero—my, mine
michnu—to crush
milnu—to fit, resemble, suit
mit—friend
mitho—edible, good to eat
morhā—stool
murkha—fool
mukh—mouth, face
mukhiā—village headman
mul—chief, main
mul bāto—main road
mul pāni—spring of water
muro—log of wood
musā—mouse

N

na—neg., particle used with participles and imperatives
na—emphasises imperatives (L. 30)
na...na—neither...nor
nāngnu—to jump over, cross
nāphā—profit
naramāilo—unhappy
narāmro—bad, ugly
nās—destruction
natro—otherwise
ni—surely, of course
niāno—warm (of body) (L. 30)
nibhāunu—to extinguish (tr.)
nibhinu—to be extinguished (intr.)
nińd—sleep
nidhāunu—to sleep
nilnu—to swallow
ko nimti—in order to
ko nimtā māń—with a view to (L. 4)
nira—near
nirbalio—weak
niskinu—to come out, get out
nisse—certainly (L. 52)
niuń—pretence, excuse
nokari—service
nuhāunu—to wash (intr.) of the body

O

ochiān—bedding
oho !—exclamation of surprise
okati—medicine
ona—termination emphasising imperatives (L. 30)
orhlānu—to come (go) down, descend (L. 39)

P

pachi—behind, after (L. 26)
pachāri—behind
pahāri—of the hills, hillman
paisā—money
pakāunu—to cook
pāl—tent

pāli—time, occasion
pālnu—to look after, cherish
(polite) to come, to go
paltan—regiment
paltāunu—to cause to overbalance
paltinu—to overbalance
pani—also, even if, in spite of (L. 29)
pāni—water
para—beyond, over there
para para—far away
parāl—straw
parkhāl—wall (temporary)
pāri—the other side (of something linear)
parhnu—to read
parnu—to be necessary, must (L. 37)
pārnu—to make (L. 50)
parsi—the day after tomorrow
pasal—shop
pasale—shopkeeper
pasnu—to enter
pasu—animal
pathāunu—to send, to cause (L. 24)
patiāunu—to believe
patni—wife
pāunā—guest
pāunu—to get, receive, find, be able (L. 24)
pauri khelnu, paurnu—to swim
pesgi—advance of money
phailāunu—to spread out (tr.)
phailinu—to spread out, extend (intr.)
phal phul—fruit
phan phan—in circles (L. 58)
phāṅt—plain, flat country
pharkinu—to turn round, return
phed—foot (of tree or hill, etc.)
phelā pārnu—to come across, find
pheri—again
phor—dirt, filth
phornu—to break (tr.)
phuknu—to blow
phul—flower
phul bāri—flower garden
phurti—smartness
phurti garnu—to be smart
phuta—suddenly (L. 57)
phutnu—to break (into pieces) (intr.), explode
piche—every
pilo—boil, abscess
pitho—flour
po—emphatic particle (L. 28)
poko—parcel
polnu—to burn, scorch, destroy by burning (L. 40)
por—last year
postak—book
pothi—female bird
prem—love
pri pri—sound of rain beginning (L. 58)
pugnu—to reach, suffice
puṅro—about (of time) (L. 48)
purāno—old (of things)
purāunu—to cause to reach
pwānkh—quill

R

ra—and (L. 30, 55)
rahanu—to remain, to continue (L. 24)
raichha—is (L. 17)
rākhnu—to place, put

rakrut—recruit
ramāilo—happy
ramāunu—to be happy
rāmro—good, beautiful
rāni—queen
rāp—heat from fire
rāri—blanket
rāt—night
e ratai !—exclamation of surprise
rāti—at night
re—used at end of sentence to indicate information received (L. 30)
rekhā—(marked) line
rin dinu—to lend
rin linu—to borrow
ris—anger
risāunu, ris garnu—to be angry
roknu—to stop
ropnu—to plant
roti—bread
rukh—tree

S

sabai—all
sābās !—well done!
sadhaiṅ—always
sadhārnu—to correct
sahanu—to endure (climate etc.)
sakdo bhar—as much as possible (L. 50)
saknu—to be able, to finish (L. 24)
sāl—year
salami—sloping
salkinu—to become alight (L. 40)
salkāunu—to set alight (L. 40)
samma—flat ground, flat
samma (sama)—up to, until (L. 26)
samātnu—to catch, grab
samāunu—to hold, seize
samjhinu—to think, understand
sancha—comfort
sāṅcho—key
sang, sanga—with, in company with
sangi—a friend
sankā mānnu—to doubt
sāno, siāno—small
sāṅs—breath
santalā—orange
sapanā dekhnu—to dream
sār—town
sārai—very
sarkār—government
sarnu—to be moved, to move (intr.)
sārnu—to move (tr.)
saruā bethā—infectious disease
sātā—week
sāta māṅ (ko)—in exchange for (L. 47)
sātha māṅ (ko)—in company with (L. 48)
sātnu—to exchange (L. 47)
sazā—punishment
selāunu—to become cold, to cool down
seo—apple
seto, sieto—white
shikār khelnu—to hunt, go shooting
siāl—jackal
siāṅthai—immediately, quickly (L. 57)
sidhārnu—to depart, set out
sidāunu—to finish (tr.) (L. 25)
sidinu—to be finished (L. 25)
sikāunu—to teach

siknu—to learn
silika—sleek, smart (L. 58)
sipāhi—soldier
sipālo—adept, expert
sist linu—to aim
sit—dew
sita—with, to (L. 47)
sital—cool, shade
sitimiti—generally (L. 56)
siunu—to sew
sobham—farewell (L. 57)
sochnu—to consider
sodhnu—to ask
soharnu—to sweep up
sor—sound, voice
sukha—comfort
sunnu—to hear, listen
surtā—sadness
surtā lāgnu—to be sad
suruāl—trousers
sutnu—to lie down
swāng pārnu—to act, pretend (L. 58)
swāsni—woman, wife

T

ta—then, therefore
tā—indeed
ta ni—surely, of course (L. 30)
tabaka—immediately, quickly (L. 57)
tāhā—information, knowledge
tāhā dinu—to inform
tāhā pāunu—to ascertain, to know (L. 38)
tāhā hunu—to know (L. 38)
tahāṅ—there
taiyār—ready
tāknu—to aim
tala—below
tālā—padlock
talab—pay
tambu—tent
taṅ—you (2nd person sing.)
tānā bānā—equipment
tāngnu—to pitch (a tent)
tānnu—to pull, stretch
tapāiṅ—you (polite) (L. 13)
tāpnu—to warm (of body) (L. 35)
tāro—far, distant
tarkāunu—to avoid
tarnu—to cross
tārnu—to take across
tarsinu—to be afraid
tarsāunu—to frighten
tatāunu—to heat, make hot
tātinu—to become hot
tāto—hot
tāuko—head
tero—your
teso, testo, tesari—like that, in that manner
thailo—bag
thaiṅ—at the house (place) of (L. 47)
thakān—arrangement
thālnu—to begin
thānnu—to think, ponder, contemplate
thānt—swagger (L. 58)
thānt pārnu—to swagger
thāplo—top of head, skull
thāpnu—to present, put forwar
thāuṅ—place
thelnu—to push
thes khānu—to stumble
thik—correct
thok—thing

thoknu—to hit
thu !—exclamation of disgust (L. 57)
thuknu—to spit
thulo—big
thuprāunu—to collect, stack (tr.)
thuprinu—to collect (intr.)
thupari, (*thupro*)—a collection
thunnu—to shut, block
tiāṅkai—exactly (L. 57)
timi (*haru*)—you
timro—your
tio—that (L. 45)
tira—direction, towards
tirkhā—thirst
tirkhā lāgnu—to be thirsty
tirnu—to pay, pay for
tiro—fare
tithā—boy, young man
toknu—to bite
topi—hat
tunikhel—parade ground
tuppa—top (of hill, etc.), summit
turanta—immediately
tusāro—frost

U

u—he
ubhinu—to stand
ubrinu—to be left over
uchinu—to overtake, outstrip
udās—anxiety
ughārnu—to open (tr.)
ughrinu—to be or become open (intr.)
uile—formerly.
umbho—up, upwards (L. 47)
umkinu—to escape (by running or jumping)
umrinu—to grow
undho—down, downwards (L. 47)
uni (*haru*)—they
upranta—besides (L. 47)
usko—his
utā—to there, thither
uthāunu—to raise, wake up (tr.)
uthnu—to rise, get up (intr.)
utranu—to descend by jumping, to get off (L. 39)
utro—as big as that
uti, *utti*—as many as that

W

wahāṅ—there
wāri—this side of (something linear)

Y

yahāṅ—here
yāne, *yāni*—that is to say
yo—this (L. 45)
yotā—one (numeral)

Z

zamin—land

VOCABULARY

English to Nepali

v. = verb. intr. = intransitive. tr. = transitive. interj. = interjection. inter. = interrogative. adv. = adverb. L = Lesson. E = Eastern form.

A

able, to be—*saknu—pāunu* (L. 24)
about, (concerning)—*ko bāri māñ*
about, of time—*puñro* (L. 48)
about to—*āñtyo* (L. 50)
above—*māñthi*
accept, (believe) (v.)—*mānnu*
account—*hisāp*
ache (v.)—*dukhnu*
act, make belief (v.)—*swāng pārnu* (L. 58)
add (v.)—*jornu*
admiration (interj.)—*āhā !* (L. 57)
advance, increase (intr.)—*barhnu* (L. 32)
advance (of money)—*pesgi*
after—*pachi* (L. 26)
afraid, to be (v.)—*tarsinu*
again—*pheri*
aim (v.)—*sist linu, tāknu*
alive—*jiuñdo*
all—*sabai*
allow (v.)—*dinu* (L. 24)
also—*pani*
always—*sadhaiñ*
among—*madde māñ*
and—*ra, ani* (L. 30, 55)
and then—*ani kheri*
anger—*ris*
angry, to be (v.)—*risāunu, ris garnu*
animal—*pasu*
animal, male—*dhāngo* (of some animals)
animal, female—*chāuri* (of some animals)
annoyance (interj.)—*hat teri !*
answer—*juāp*
ant—*kamilā-kimlā*
anxiety—*udās*
apple—*seo*
application (written)—*binti patra*
applied, to be (v.)—*lāgnu* (L. 33)
apply (v.)—*lāunu—lagāunu* (L. 33)
approval—*manjuri*
arrangement—*thakān*
arrive (v.)—*āipugnu*
arrow—*kāñr*
as—*jhaiñ, jasto*
ashamed, to be (v.)—*lāj lāgnu (lāi)*
ask (v.)—*sodhnu*
astonish (v.) (tr.)—*dangai pārnu*
astonished, to be (v.)—(intr.)—*dangai hunu*

at—*mān* (*ma*)
attack (v.)—*chopnu*
attention, to pay (v.)—*dhiān dinu*
avoid—*tarkāunu*

B

bad—*narāmro*
bag—*thailo*
balcony—*kāusi*
ball—*goli*
bang, to make a (v.)—*diānghai pārnu*
be (v.)—*hunu* (L. 16)
beautiful—*rāmro*
because—*bhanera* (L. 34)
kina bhanie (L. 56)
bed—*khāt*
bedding—*ochiān*
bee—*māuri*
before—*agāri, aghi*
begin (v.)—*lāgnu* (L. 33) *thālnu*
begin, to cause to (v.)—*lāunu* (L. 33)
behaviour—*chāl*
behind—*pachi, pachāri*
believe (v.)—*patiāunu*
below—*tala*
besides—*upranta* (L. 47)
bewilder (v.)—*hairān pārnu*
big—*thulo*
big, how (inter.)—*katro*
as big as—*jatro*
as big as this—*etro*
as big as that—*utro*
bird—*charā*
,, male—*bhāle*
,, female—*pothi*
,, young—*challā*

bite (v.)—*toknu*
black—*kālo*
blanket—*rāri*—*kāmlo*
blindly—*andhā dhundā*
block, stop up, shut (v.)—*thunnu*
blow (v.)—*phuknu*
beat—*dungā*
boil, eruption of skin—*pilo*
bone—*hār*
book—*kitāb, postak*
boots—*juttā*
borrow (v.)—*rin linu*
bow (arrow)—*dhanu*
boy—*tithā, ketā* (E.)
branch—*hāngā*
bread—*roti*
break (v.) (intr.) (of something linear)—*bhānchnu*
(intr. into pieces)—*phutnu*
(tr.)—*phornu*
breath—*sāns*
bring (v.)—*liāunu, liera āunu, leidinu* (L. 33)
brother (elder)—*dāju*
(younger)—*bhāi*
(eldest—*jeto*
bucket—*bālti*
bullet—*goli*
burn (v.)
(intr.)—*balnu* (L. 40)
(tr.)—*bālnu* (L. 40)
(tr.)—*darnu* (L. 40)
(intr.)—*salkinu* (L. 40)
(tr.)—*salkāunu* (L. 40)
(tr.)—*polnu* (L. 40)
bush—*jhor, jhiāng*
buy (v.)—*kinnu*
by—*le*

C

calculate (v.)—*chitta pāunu* (L. 38)

call (v.)—*bolāunu*

cart—*gārā*

casualty—*ghāite*

cat—*birālu*

catch—*samāunu, samātnu*

cause to (v.)—*pathāunu* (L. 24)

certainly—*nisse, khās* (L. 52)

charitable (to be) (v.)—*baksinu* (L. 13)

chatter—*gan gan*

chatter (v.)—*gangan garnu ken ken garnu* (See Lesson 58)

chattering (a.)—*gangani*

chicken—*kukrā*

chief, main—*mul*

child—*bālakha*

children—*ketāketi*

chilli—*khursāni*

clever—*bātho*

cliff—*bhir*

climb (v.)—*charhnu*

cloth, clothes—*lugā*

cold—*jāro*

(of liquids)—*chiso*

cold, to become, cool down (v.)—*selāunu*

collapse (v.)—*bhatkinu*

collapse, to cause to (tr.)—*bhatkāunu*

collect (v.) (intr.)—*thuprinu*

(tr.)—*Thuprāunu*

come (v.)—*āunu*

come (v.) polite form—*pālnu*

come down (v.)—*orhlānu* (L. 39)

come out (v.)—*niskinu*

comfort—*sancha, sukha*

company (in company with)—*ko sātha māṅ*

competition—*bāzi*

consider, accept, obey (v.)—*mānnu*

continue (v.)—*rahanu* (L. 24)

cook—*bhānse*

cook (v.)—*pakāunu*

cookhouse, kitchen—*bhānsa chaukā*

cool, become cool, (v.)—*selāunu*

cool (of atmosphere)—*sital*

correct—*thik*

correct (v.)—*sadhārnu*

country—*des*

cow—*gāi*

coward—*kāphar*

cowherd—*gothālā*

crops—*bāli*

cross (v.) (intr.)—*tarnu, nāngnu*

cross, to take (v.) (tr.)—*tārnu*

crowd—*thupro*

crumpled—*kachang kuchung*

crush (v.)—*michnu*

cut—*chot*

cut (v)—*kātnu*

cut (causative) to cause to—*katāunu*

D

daughter—*chori*

day—*din*

today—*āju*

day after tomorrow—*parsi*

day before yesterday, the other day—*asti*

daytime—*diuṅso*

dear (of price)—*māṅgo*

decorated—*jhilli milli* (L. 58)

decrease (intr.)—*ghatinu*
(tr.)—*ghatāunu*
deep—*gairo*
deficient—*apugdo*
demand, require (v.)—*māngnu*
depart, set out (v.)—*sidhārnu*
descend (v.)—*jharnu, orhlānu*
descend (by jumping)—*ulranu* (L. 39)
destruction—*nās*
detail (v)—*khatāunu*
determined (to be) (v.)—*ānt balio garnu*
dew—*sit*
die (v.)—*marnu*
deficient—*ghati, apugdo*
dig (v)—*khannu*
direction—*tira*
dirt—*phor*
disciple, pupil—*chelā*
discomfort—*dukh*
disgust (interj.)—*e, thu, chichi* (L. 57)
divide, distribute (v.)—*bāṅrnu*
do ((v.)—*garnu*
do (causative to cause to do) (v.)—*garāunu*
dog—*kukur*
door (small)—*dailo*
(large) gate—*dhokā*
doubt (v.)—*sankā mānnu*
downwards—*undho, taltira*
dream—*sapanā dekhnu*
drink (v)—*khānu*
duck—*hāṅs*
dust—*dhulo*

E

ear—*kān*
earn (v.)—*kamāunu*
earth, soil—*māto*
eat (v.)—*khānu*
eat to satisfaction (v.)—*aghāunu*
edge (at the edge of)—*ko cheu māṅ*
edible—*mitho*
either...or—*ki...ki*
elephant—*hāthi*
enclosure—*khor*
endure (v.)—*khapnu*
(of climate, etc.)—*sahanu*
enemy—*bairi, dushman*
England—*belāet*
English—*angrezi*
enlist (v.) (tr.)—*bharti garnu*
(intr.)—*bharti hunu*
enter (v.)—*pasnu*
equipment—*tānā bāna*
escape (v.)—*umkinu*
even if—*pani* (L. 29)
evening—*beluki, beluka*
every—*sabai*
every to, with,—*piche* (follows noun)
everything—*kharang khurung* (L. 58)
everywhere—*jahāṅ sukhai* (L. 50)
exactly—*tiāṅkai* (L. 57)
except—*chāri*
exchange (v.)—*sātnu* (L. 47)
in exchange for—*ko sāta māṅ*
excuse—*niuṅ*
excuse (to make)—*niuṅ garnu*
exhausted—*lutruk, lutrukai* (L. 57)
expert—*sipālo*
explode (v.) (intr.)—*phutnu*
extinguish (v.) (tr.)—*nibhāunu*

extinguish (v.) (intr.) to be extinguished—*nibhinu*
eye—*āṅkhā*

F

face—*mukh*
fact (in fact)—*baru* (L. 55)
fall (v.) (intr.)—*larnu, khasnu*
fall, to cause to (v.) (tr.)—*khasālnu* (L. 39)
far away—*para para, tāro*
fare—*tiro*
farewell—*sobham* (L. 57)
farm—*goth*
farmer—*khetālā*
father—*bābu*
feed (v.) (tr.)—*khuāunu*
fetch (v.)—*linu jānu*
fever—*jaro*
few—*ali, ali kati*
field—*bāri*
fight (v.)—*larnu*
fill (v.)—*bharnu* (L. 32)
fill to cause to—*bharāunu* (L. 32)
find (v.)—*pāunu, phela pārnu*
finish (v.) (intr.)—*saknu* (L. 24)
(intr.)—*sidinu* (L. 25)
(tr.)—*sidāunu* (L. 25)
finish off (v.)—*hālnu*
fire—*āgo*
fit, suit (v.)—*milnu*
flat—*samma*
flat country—*phāṅt, samma, chāur*
flour—*pitho*
flower—*phul*
flower garden—*phul bāri*
food, rice—*bhāt, khāne kurā, khurāk*
fool—*baulāhā, murkha*
foot, base (of hill, tree, etc.)—*phed*
forest—*ban*
forget (v.)—*birsinu*
formerly—*uile*
friend—*sangi, mit*
frighten (v.)—*tarsāunu*
from—*bāti, bāta, bāto*
from (of time, (E.) of place)—*dekhi, dekhin*
front (in front of)—*aghi, agāri*
frost—*tusāro*
fruit—*phal phul*

G

gamble (v.)—*juā khelnu*
gate—*dhokā*
generally—*siti miti* (L. 56)
get (v.)—*pāunu*
get up (v.)—*uthnu*
gift—*dān*
give (v.)—*dinu*
go away (v.)—*jaijānu*
go (v.)—*jānu* (polite form) *pālnu*
goat—*bākrā*
goat, male—*bokhā*
goat, female—*bākri*
gobble (v.)—*khuāpai khānu*
swallow—*nilnu* (L. 57)
good—*rāmro, bes* (L. 57)
government—*sarkār*
grab (v.)—*samātnu, samāunu*
grandfather—*bāze*
ground—*bhuiṅ*
grow (v.)—*barhnu, umrinu* (L. 32)
guest—*pāunā*
Gurkha (man)—*Gurkhāli*

H

habit—*bāni*
half—*ādhā*
hand—*hāth*
happy—*ramāilo*
happy (to be) (v.)—*ramāunu*
haste—*hatār*
hat—*topi*
hate (v.)—*hin garnu*
haversack—*jholā, jholi*
hay—*khar*
he—*u*
head—*tāuko*
headman—*mukhiā*
hear, listen (v.)—*sunnu*
heat (from fire)—*rāp*
heat (v.)—*tatāunu*
help (v.)—*gohār dinu*
here—*yahāṅ*
hill—*daṅrā*
high hills—*lekh, himāl*
hillman—*pahāri*
his—*usko, tesko*
hit (v.)—*hānnu, hirkāunu, thoknu*
hither—*itā, ittā (yetā)*
hold (take in sense of holding)—*linu*
hole—*dulo*
  (open both sides)—*pawāl*
hoof—*khur*
hope—*āsā*
hope (v.)—*āsā garnu*
horse—*ghorā*
hot—*garam*
hot (of liquids)—*tāto*
hot (of body)—*niāno*
hour—*ghantā*
house—*ghar, kothā*
how much?—*kati, katti*
how? (inter.)—*kaso, kasori*
  (L. 46 & 56)—*kasogari bhanie*
  what kind of?—*kasto*
huddled together—*guju muju*
hunt (sport) (v.)—*shikār khelnu*
hut—*jhupro*

I

if—*bhanie* (L. 27)
  bha (L. 27)
  hundo ho (L. 27)
ill—*birāmi*
illness, disease—*bethā*
immediately—*siāṅtai* (L. 57)
  tabaka (L. 57)
  turanta (L. 57)
in—*māṅ, ma*
increase (v.) (intr.)—*barhnu* (L. 32)
  (tr.)—*barhāunu*
indeed—*tā*
infectious disease—*saruā bethā*
inform (v.)—*tāhā dinu*
information—*tāhā*
insect—*kirā*
inside—*bhitra*
intelligent—*chaṅkhie, bātho*

J

jackal—*siāl*
jail—*jhel khāna*
jealous—*dāhi*
jungle—*jangal*
jump over, cross (v.)—*nāngnu*
just (adv.)—*bharkar* (L. 51)

K

key—*sāṅcho*
kill (v.)—*mārnu*
knot—*gāṅtho*

know (v.)—*jānnu* (L. 24, 38)
tāhā hunu (L. 38)
tāhā pāunu (L. 38)
(who knows?)—*koni*

L

ladder (European style)—
bhariāng
(single notched pole)—*lisnu*
lame—*larang lurung* (L. 58)
land—*zamin*
language—*kurā*
at last—*balla*
late—*abelā, bher*
lazy—*luthro*
learn (v.)—*siknu*
leave—*bidā, chutti*
leave (v.)—*chārnu*
leech—*jugā*
left—*debre, bāheṅ*
lend (v.)—*rin dinu*
lie down (v.)—*sutnu*
like (rel.)—*jaso, jasto, jasori,*
jhaiṅ (L. 43)
like this—*eso, esto, esari*
like that—*teso, testo, tesari*
limb—*bāhāṅ*
line—*lang*
(marked)—*rekhā*
little (quantity)—*ali, ali kati*
(small)—*sāno, siāno*
live (v.)—*basnu*
load (of baggage etc.) (v)—*lādnu*
load (to cause to)—*ladāunu*
log (of wood)—*muro*
long—*lāmo*
look (v.)—*hernu*
look after, watch over (v.)—
herchār garnu, pālnu
lose (a game, battle) (v.)—*hārnu*
(misplace)—*harāunu*
love—prem

M

make, prepare, etc. (v.)—
banāunu, pārnu (L. 50)
make a mistake (v.)—*birāunu*
man, person—*mānchhe, logne*
many—*dherai* (L. 43)
how many (inter.)—*kati, katti*
as many as—*jati, jatti*
as many at this—*eti, etti*
as many as that—*uti, utti*
marry (v.)—*bihā garnu*
married, to be (v.)—*bihā hunu*
measles—*dādura*
meat—*māsu*
medicine—*āusatai, okati*
meet (v.)—*bhetnu, bhetāunu*
meet, to cause to (v.)—*bhetāunu*
mind—*man*
mind (take exception to) (v.)—
dhandā mānnu
moment—*chin*
one moment—*ek chin*
money—*paisā*
month—*mahina*
more—*āru*
more, all the more—*jhan* (L. 44)
moreover—*ani*
morning—*bihān*
,, in the morning—*bihāno*
mother—*āmā*
mouse—*musā*
mouth—*mukh*
move (v.) (intr.)—*halinu*
move (tr.)—*halāunu*
move (from one place to
another (intr.)—*sarnu*
(tr.)—*sārnu*
movement—*harkat*
much (too much)—*barhdā* (L. 32)
mud—*hilo*

must (v.)—*parnu* (L. 37)
my—*mero*

N

near—*nira*
nearly—*jhandai*
necessary, to be (v.)—*parnu* (L. 37)
necessary (an object)—*chāhinchha* (L. 37)
neither—nor—*na...na*
never—*kaile pani* (L. 43)
night—*rāt*
at night—*rāti*
no—*ahan* (L. 58)
noise—*khalbal, "dadang ra dudung"* (L. 58)
none—*kei, koi* (L. 45)
not at all—*chattai* (L. 52)
nothing—*kei pani*
notice (v.)—*chāl pāunu* (L. 38)
now—*aile*
nowadays—*hijo āju*

O

obey (v.)—*mānnu*
office—*daftar*
oh! (when in pain)—*aiyu!* (L. 57)
old (thing)—*purāno*
old man—*burho*
old woman—*burhi*
on—*mān* (*ma*), *mānthi*
one (the one)—*chain, chāine* (L. 55)
one (numeral)—*yotā*
only—*mātrai*
open (v.) (tr.)—*ughārnu*
open, to be (intr.)—*ughrinu*
or—*ki* (L. 4)
orange—*santalā*
order (v.)—*hukam dinu, arhāunu*
order (in order to)—*bhanera* (L. 34)
,, —*lāi* (L. 48)
,, —*ko lāgi* (L. 48)
,, —*ko nimti* (L. 47)
,, —*ko nimtā mān* (L. 47)
other—*ārko*
others—*āru*
other side of—*pāri*
this side of—*wāri*
otherwise—*natro*
ought—*chāhinchha* (L. 37)
our—*hamro*
outside—*bāira*
over balance (v.)—*paltinu*
,, ,, (to cause to)—*paltāunu*
overtake (v.)—*uchinu*
over there, further—*para*
own—*āphnu*

P

padlock—*tālā*
parade—*kawāz*
parade ground—*tunikhel*
parcel, bundle—*guntā, poko*
pay—*talab, khānki*
pay (v.), pay for—*tirnu*
person—*mānchhe, janā*
pipe (smoking)—*hukka*
pit—*khālto*
pitch (a tent) (v.)—*tāngnu*
place—*thāun*
plain (flat country)—*chāur, phānt*
plant (crops, flowers, etc.) (v.)—*ropnu*
play (v.)—*khelnu*
please—*hawas, holā* (L. 13)

polish (v.)—*malnu*
poor—*kaṅgāli*
potato—*ālu*
pour (v.)—*khaniāunu*
present, submit, (cause to mount) (v.)—*charhāunu, Thāpnu*
pretence—*niuṅ*
probably—*holā* (L. 11)
profit—*nāphā*
promise (v.)—*karahār garnu*
pull (v.)—*tānnu*
punishment—*sazā*
punish (v.)—*sazā dinu*
pupil—*chelā*
purpose (for the purpose of)—*ko nimti, ko khātir le*
put—place (v.)—*rākhnu*
push—*thelnu*

Q

queen—*rāni*
quickly—*chito, chāṅro, jhatta siāṅtai, tabaka,* etc. (L. 57)
quiet—*chām chum*
quill—*pwānkh*

R

rain (v.)—*pāni parnu*
,, (heavily)—*pāni darara āunu* (L. 58)
,, (lightly)—*pāni pripri āunu* (L. 58)
rainy season, monsoon—*barkhā*
raise (v.)—*uthāunu*
reach (v.)—*pugnu*
reach, to cause to—*purāunu*
read (v.)—*parhnu*
ready—*taiyār*
real—*khās*
reason—*kāran, hunā le* (L. 47)
receive, get (v.)—*pāunu*
recognise (v.)—*chinnu* (L. 38)
recruit—*rakrut*
regiment—*paltan*
relief—*badlā*
remain (v.) *rahanu* (L. 24)
remain (v.) to be left over—*ubrinu*
reprimand—*ghurki*
reproof—*dhamki*
resemble (v.)—*milnu*
retreat (v.)—*hatnu*
return (v.)—*gaera āunu, pharkinu, pharkera āunu*
rice (growing)—*dhān*
,, (before cooking)—*chāṅwal*
,, (cooked)—*bhāt*
rice beer—*jāṅr*
rich—*dhani*
riches—*dhan*
rise (v.)—*uthnu*
,, (of sun)—*jhulkinu*
river—*kholā*
road—*bāto*
,, (main)—*mul bāto*
room—*kothā*
rot (v.)—*kuhunu, makinu*
run (v.)—*dugurnu, dāurnu*
run away (v.)—*bhāgnu*

S

sack—*borā, bori*
sadness—*surtā*
sad, to be (v.)—*surtā lāgnu*
save (rescue) (v.)—*bachāunu*
saved (to be) (v.)—*bachnu*
save, earn (money, etc.) (v.)—*kamāunu*
say (v.)—*bhannu*

scorch (v.)—*polnu* (L. 40)
search (to search for) (v.)—
khojnu
seedling, sapling—*biruwā*
see (v.)—*dekhnu*
self—*āphu, āphai* (L. 45)
send (v.)—*pathāunu*
separate—*alag*
separate (v.)—*chutāunu*
servant—*chākar*
service—*nokari, chākari*
in service—*bharti bhāko*
set (of sun)—*astāunu*
sew (v.)—*siunu*
shade—*chāen*
shallow—*chip chipe*
sharpen (v.) (tr.)—*dhār pārnu*
sharp, to be (v.) (intr.)—*dhār*
lāgnu
shoe—*juttā*
shop—*pasal*
shopkeeper—*pasale*
shortly—*bholi parsi*
shoulder—*kum*
shout (v.)—*karāunu*
show (v.) (by explanation)—
batāunu
,, (by pointing out)—
dekhāunu
shut, stop up (v.)—*thunnu*
since—*dekhi, dekhin*
sister (elder)—*didi*
,, (younger)—*bdini*
sit (v.)—*basnu*
sit, to cause to (v.)—*basālnu*
skull—*thāplo*
sleep—*nind*
sleep (v.)—*nidhāunu*
sloping—*salāmi*
slowly—*bistāro, bistārai*

small—*sāno, siāno*
smashed—*kamlang. kumlung*
(L. 58)
smart—*silika* (L. 58)
smart, to be (v.)—*phurti garnu*
smoke (v.) of tobacco—*khānu*
snow—*hiun*
soldier—*sipāhi*
somebody—*koi, kasai* (Agent
case) (L. 45)
someone or other—*koi na koi*
(L. 52)
something or other—*kei na kei*
(L. 52)
sometime ago—*hijo asti*
son—*choro*
soon, quickly—*chānro*
soon, as soon as—*bittikai* (L. 48)
sort, what sort of?—*kasto ?*
sorry (sad) to be (v.)—*surtā*
lāgnu
sound—*sor*
sow (seed) (v.)—*charnu*
speak (v.)—*bolnu*
spit—*thuknu*
spite, in spite of—*pani* (L. 29)
split (v.) (tr.)—*chirnu*
spread out, extend (v.) (intr.)—
phailinu
(tr.)—*phailāunu*
spring (of water)—*mul pāni*
stand (v.)—*ubhinu*
stay (the night) (v.)—*bās basnu*
steal (v.)—*chornu*
still, yet—*ajha* (L. 43, 55)
stone—*dhungā*
stool—*morhā*
stop (v.) (tr.)—*roknu*
stores—*māl*
story—*kathā*

straw—*parāl*
strike, hit (v.)—*hānnu, thoknu*
,, the hour—*bajnu*
strong—*balio*
stumble (v.)—*thes khānu*
suddenly—*phuta* (L. 57)
suffice (to) (v.)—*pugnu*
sun, rays—*ghām*
Sunday—*āitwār*
surely—*ni, ta ni* (L. 30)
surprise (interj.)—*abui ! bābā ! amai ! ratai ! oho !* (L. 57)
Note initial "*a*" is short.
suit (v.)—*milnu*
swallow (v.)—*nilnu*
swaying—*ghamlang ghumlung*
sweep up, (v.)—*soharnu* (L. 58)

T

take away (v.)—*lagnu, lejānu* (L. 33)
take, hold (v.)—*linu* (L. 33)
take with (v.)—*lānu* (L. 33)
talk, speech, language—*kurā*
talk (v.)—*bolnu, kurā garnu*
tall—*ālko*
tea—*chiā*
teach (v.)—*sikāunu*
tell (v.)—*bhannu*
temple (shrine)—*deota thān*
tent—*pāl, tambu*
than—*bhandā, dekhi* (L. 42)
that (pronoun)—*tio* (L. 45)
that (conjunction)—*bhanera* (L. 34)
then—*ta*
there—*tahāṅ, wahāṅ*
therefore—*ta*
they—*ini (haru) uni (haru)*
thing—*kurā, thok*
think (v.)—*samjhinu, sochnu, thānnu*
thirst—*tirkhā*
thirsty, to be (v.)—*tirkhā lāgnu*
this—*yo* (L. 45)
thither—*utā*
Thursday—*bibār*
tighten (v.)—*kasnu*
time—*belā* (L. 15)
,, (period)—*kher* (L. 15)
,, (once, twice, three times etc.)—*pāli* (L. 7)
to (dative)—*lāi*
of place—*māṅ*
tomorrow—*bholi*
top (of hill)—*tuppa*
towards—*tira*
town—*sār*
tree—*rukh*
trouble—*dukha*
trousers—*suruāl*
try (v.)—*khojnu*
turn round (v.)—*pharkinu*

U

ugly—*narāmro*
understand (v.)—*bujhnu*
unhappy—*naramāilo*
until—*samma, sama* (L. 26)
up to, on a level with—*samma (sama)*
upwards—*umbho, māttira, māstira*

V

valley—*kholsā*
various—*anek*
very—*dherai, bahatai, bignai, chaupatai, aghorai, sārai* (L. 43)
via—*bāro*
village—*gāuṅ*

W

wake up (v.) (intr.)—*biuṅjhinu*
(tr.)—*uthāunu*

(Note *jāgnu* and *jagāunu* are not true Nepali)

walk (v.)—*hiṅrnu*

wall—*bhittā*

,, (temporary)—*parkhāl*

wander, go for a walk (v.)—*dulnu, ghumnu*

want (v.)—*chāhinchha*
(with a verb) *man lāgnu* (L. 37)

war—*dhāuwa, larāi*

warm—*tato, garam*
of atmosphere or body—*niāno*

warm (v.) of body—*tāpnu*
,, to make hot—*tatāunu*

wash, body (v.) (intr.)—*nuhāunu*

wash (v.) (tr.)—*dhunu*

watch (v.)—*hernu*

water—*pāni*

we—*hami, hamiharu*

weak—*nirbalio*

wear (v.)—*lāunu* (L. 33)

Wednesday—*budhbār*

week—*sātā*

well (adverb)—*besri*

well done (interj.)—*sābās*

wet (cold of liquids)—*chiso*

what? (inter.)—*ke, kie* (L. 30)

whatever (relative)—*je* (L. 45)

when? (inter.)—*kaile*

when (relative)—*jaba, jaile* (L. 43)

where? (inter.)—*kahāṅ, khoi*
(relative)—*jahāṅ* (L. 43)
,, —*kāṅ, thaiṅ* (L. 47)

whether—*bhanera* (L. 34)

which—*kun* (L. 46)

whichever—*jun* (L. 43)

while—*kheri* (L. 15)

whither? (inter.)—*katā* (L. 4)
(relative)—*jatā* (L. 43)

white—*seto, sieto*

who?—*ko* (L. 46)
(relative)—*jo* (L. 46)

whole—*bhari* (L. 32)

whose? (inter.)—*kasko*
(relative)—*jasko*

why?—*kina, ke lāi* (L. 45)

wife—*swāsni, patni*

win (v.)—*jitnu*

wind—*batās*

window—*jhiāl*

winter—*hiuṅdo*

witch—*boksi*

with—*sang, sanga, sita* (L. 47)
sātha māṅ (L. 48)

woman—*āimāi*
swāsni

wood—*kāth*
fuel—*dāurā*

work—*kām*

wound—*ghāu*

wounded—*ghail bhāko*

wreck (v.)—*busukhai pārnu* (L. 57)

write (v.)—*lekhnu*

Y

year—*barkha, barsa, sāl*
(next year)—*āghuṅ*
(last year)—*por*

yes—*aṅ, ho*

yesterday—*hijo, hiju*

yet, not yet—*ajha* (L. 43, 55)

you—*taṅ, timi*
āphu, tapāiṅ, hazur (L. 13)

your—*tero, timro*

young—*kalilo*